T0204287

The Charles River

The Charles River

Exploring
Nature and History
on Foot and by Canoe

Ron McAdow

Illustrated by
Gordon Morrison

Bliss Publishing Company, Inc.,
P.O. Box 920, Marlborough, Massachusetts 01752

The quotation on page 81 from "The Morse Mills at South
Natick" written by Marion Pfeiffer in 1959, is used with permission of her daughter, Hester Pfeiffer Klie. The excerpt on
page 83, from Volume II of *Birds of Massachusetts and Other
New England States* by Edward H. Forbush, Copyright 1927 by
the Commonwealth of Massachusetts, is used with permission
of Greg Watson, Commissioner of the Massachusetts
Department of Food and Agriculture.

Published 1992. First edition

98 97 96 95 94 93 92   5 4 3 2

Library of Congress Cataloging-in-Publication Data

McAdow, Ron, 1949 -

    The Charles River: Exploring nature and history
on foot and by canoe / by Ron McAdow; illustrations
by Gordon Morrison.

Includes bibliographical references (p. 210) and index.
ISBN 0-9625144-1-1
1. Outdoor recreation — Massachusetts — Charles River
Region — Guide-books. 2. Canoes and canoeing —
Massachusetts — Charles River Region — Guide-books.
3. Charles River Region (Mass.) — History — Guide-books.
4. Charles River Region (Mass.) — Description and travel —
Guide-books. I. Title.
GV191.42.M4M38 1991
790'.09744'4 — dc20

                                                91-21450
                                                CIP

ISBN 0-9625144-1-1

Graphic Design by Christine Anderson
Cover illustration by Gordon Morrison ©

PRINTED IN THE UNITED STATES OF AMERICA
Bliss Publishing Company, Inc.
P.O. Box 920, Marlborough, Massachusetts 01752

To Deborah

*On a long journey, a sturdy partner
is a blessing. It is my good fortune
to share the work and the fun
with a strong paddler.*

CONTENTS

Charles River Towns

MAPS

Coming out of town, willingly as usual,
when I saw that reach of the Charles River
just above the depot, the fair still water this
cloudy evening suggesting the way to eternal
peace and beauty. The placid, lake-like fresh
water, so unlike the salt brine, affected me
not a little. This is perhaps the first vision of
elysium on this route from Boston. And just
then I saw an encampment of Penobscots,
their wigwams appearing above the railroad
fence, they, too, looking up the river as they
sat on the ground, and enjoying the scene.
What can be more impressive than to look up
a noble river just at evening, one, perchance,
which you have never explored, and behold
its placid waters reflecting the woods and
sky, lapsing inaudibly toward the ocean; to
behold it as a lake, but know it as a river,
tempting the beholder to explore it and his
own destiny at once?

(from the journal of Henry David Thoreau,
July 9, 1851)

Introduction

On the afternoon of February 21, 1676 two hundred native warriors roasted an ox on a hill overlooking the Charles River. Across the river smoke rose from dozens of points scattered over the Medfield landscape. At the foot of the hill, flames licked the timbers spanning the Charles. Metacomet's fighters had burned the English bridge. For them there would be no more peaceful coexistence with the newcomers; it was a struggle to the death. At the time of the Medfield battle, the Indians were winning the war, and the colonists felt that their survival was in doubt. Mendon and Wrentham, Charles River towns farther inland than Medfield, were among fifty settlements destroyed during the war by Metacomet, called King Philip by the English.

Thirty years earlier a Puritan minister named John Eliot had taken it upon himself to reach out to the natives of Massachusetts. He first preached to Waban's people near the Charles in Newton, and established a new town for Indians, called Natick, which straddled the river. Though determined to convert them to his religion, Eliot's approach to the Indians was respectful. He mastered their language, and he did his best for them, by his own lights, for all of his long life. In the darkest hour of King Philip's War it was Eliot's converts, recalled from wartime internment on a Boston Harbor island, who brought guerrilla warfare skills that helped the English survive Metacomet's challenge.

Dozens of Medfield's survivors owed their lives to a stone house near the mouth of Bogastow Brook, the largest tributary of the Charles. They took refuge there during the February battle, and again during a second attack in May. It is possible today to park an automobile near the site of that garrison house, to put a canoe onto the pond there, and to paddle to the Charles. In the course of a leisurely day's travel, canoeists will float past the site of the ox-roast and the remains of Death's Bridge, where the native fighters posted a written warning to the English. After landing at Rocky Narrows, lunch can be eaten in the cool shade of hemlocks before a hike up to King Philip's Lookout, to survey the valley of the Charles. The afternoon will be spent on the river's most rural section where there is every chance of seeing a hawk or a great blue heron. Late in the day the canoe arrives in the village of South Natick, which was John

Eliot's first and most successful Indian town.

The Charles River has always been at the heart of Massachusetts. To understand one, it is necessary to know something of the other. This book is a venture in learning about both. Part One is a guide to the Charles and its tributaries for paddlers, walkers, and armchair explorers. Like most river trips it follows the current, beginning at the source of the Charles in Hopkinton and descending to Boston Harbor. Part Two tells the story of the settlement of Massachusetts Bay, and recounts some aspects of later history that pertain to the Charles. Massachusetts began at the mouth of the river and crept upstream, and so the story of settlement is recounted town by town from Boston to the headwaters.

The Charles boasts a rich industrial history. Massachusetts was settled by farmers, but its rocky soil could not support a large population. After the American Revolution many farmers moved to the Ohio Valley, but the mechanically inclined found much to do along the Charles because manufacturing and railroads formed a new economic base. In the early 1800s, industrial mills were built at every fall of the river. The first steam railroad to open service in Massachusetts was the Boston and Worcester. Its primitive engines puffed across a trestle spanning that part of the Charles' estuary called the Back Bay. The Boston and Worcester Railroad changed the river towns. It opened the farms of Brookline, Newton, Weston, and Wellesley to settlement by suburbanites, brought industry to Natick, and eventually carried enough of Needham to Boston to make the Back Bay into dry land. In its mastery of cutting-edge technology the Puritan Commonwealth found its economic future, symbolized on the Charles by the Massachusetts Institute of Technology, which occupies a filled-in salt marsh on the north bank.

As the pat answers of the Puritan fathers yielded to questions, explorations of a social and spiritual nature also took place along the Charles. During the 1840s a group led by a former Unitarian minister moved to Brook Farm in West Roxbury. The Brook Farmers sought greater harmony with each other and the Earth. In the same era "practical Christian socialism" was tried far upstream at Hopedale.

The natural beauty of the river has long been appreciated for its recreational, restorative value. In the early years of the twentieth century boat houses on the

Charles stored thousands of wood-and-canvas canoes, ready for launch when their owners rode the electric railroads out from the city.

The river traveller encounters a host of plants and animals on and along the Charles, and some of the most characteristic and interesting of these are described in comments on "study areas," which are places on the river especially worthy of visiting because of their natural or historical assets. The designation of these as study areas is a plan for the future rather than a fact from the past, and readers are invited to take part in recording the natural history of these areas. Notes sent to the author will be accumulated for reference by naturalists of the future.

Key to River Maps

Basin Location

WALTHAM
WATERTOWN
CAMBRIDGE
136 142 148 154
WESTON
128
NEWTON
120
BROOKLINE
BOSTON
WELLESLEY
100
NEEDHAM
108
NATICK
88 104
DEDHAM
SHERBORN
76
DOVER
WESTWOOD
HOPKINTON
72 66
MEDFIELD
page 6
HOLLISTON
MILFORD
52
MEDWAY
MILLIS
62
12
40
28
HOPEDALE
16
36
48
NORFOLK
20
MENDON
FRANKLIN
WRENTHAM
BELLINGHAM

0   5 mi

Part One:
A Guide to the
Charles River

How to Use This Guide

River Sections

Each river section contains a topographic map, a description of access points, commentary, and a list of suggested outings. Some sections also have notes about study areas where observations of nature or traces of the past are particularly rewarding.

The background maps are composites of United States Geological Survey (USGS) topographic quadrangles. The reproductions used here are slightly reduced, to a scale consistent throughout. These recent USGS topographic maps show elevations in meters. Unlike their predecessors which were sold as flat sheets, the new metric maps are folded and double-sized; each contains two of the old quadrangles. In the description of the access points, the USGS map named refers to these new, folded, double-sized maps.

To feel comfortable and confident in outdoor explorations the single most important step is to obtain topographic maps and to understand and use the information they contain. Learning to decipher these maps takes time and practice, but once mastered both the danger and the fear of becoming lost are greatly diminished. Each contour line represents a three-meter difference in elevation. Every fifth line is darker, indicating intervals of fifteen meters between the dark contour lines, which are marked with their altitudes. Fifteen meters is approximately fifty feet; to convert meters to feet, multiply by 3.2808.

In order to reach the access points by automobile, good road maps will be useful; the maps of river sections are not intended to suffice for this purpose.

In the commentary about the river sections, right and left are used in preference to compass directions to indicate which side of the river something is on. Because the Charles meanders toward every point of the compass, reference to the direction of flow is more helpful to the canoeist. Right and left always refer to someone facing downstream.

Where to Begin

To find a particular kind of outing, refer to the Suggested Outings Directory on page 201. To plan a visit to a particular place, begin with the key map on the first page of this section. In either case you will be referred to one of twenty-three sections of the Charles or its tributaries. Outings on foot generally begin and end at a parking lot or public transportation station. Canoe trips require a little more forethought.

How to Plan a Canoe Day Trip

The simplest plan for a canoe outing is to go to a waterside canoe livery. For a modest fee you will be equipped with boat, paddle, and personal flotation device (formerly called a life jacket), and put onto the water next to the establishment. On the Charles River this could be the Charles River Canoe and Kayak Service, from which you can explore the Lakes District, paddle upstream to Lower Falls, or paddle downstream to the Moody Street Dam in Waltham. Charles River canoeists also hire boats from Upriver Outfitters at Millis, which serves the middle of the river. To enjoy such an outing, take along a cheerful companion, a hat that will not blow off easily, sunscreen, sunglasses, and a picnic lunch. This kind of canoeing has long been associated with courtship, especially at the Lakes District, where at the turn of the century it was thought necessary to have rules against undue displays of affection.

Another plan for a day trip uses an automobile to transport the canoe to the location of choice. The canoe must be firmly attached to the roof of the car. Here is an effective way to do this.

How to Secure a Canoe to an Automobile

Equipment:
> 2 car-top bars
> 4 foam gunnel pads (gunnels are the rims of a canoe's sides)
> 4 nylon straps with toothed clasps

Step 1: Attach the car-top bars to the automobile.

Step 2: Put the canoe, upside down, onto the car-top bars. Make sure that the bars stick out several inches on each side of the canoe.

Step 3: Put one of the foam gunnel pads on the gunnel at each place it crosses the car-top bars. This protects the finish of the gunnel and reduces the likelihood that the canoe will slip from side to side.

Step 4: Fasten the canoe to the car-top bars with two of the nylon straps. Pull them as tight as you can. At this point the canoe is pretty well attached to the car, but the stresses of starting and stopping, turning, and wind can be sudden and strong, so it is wise to go further.

Step 5: Secure the ends of the canoe, using the towing eyes beneath the car. The nylon strap will form a triangle. If long straps are not available, nylon rope can be used instead. It is important to use a material that will stretch a bit, to keep the canoe under tension.

What to Take

Casual paddlers need only personal flotation devices (life jackets), sun protection, paddles, and a boat. But for journeys of exploration you should take along a kit that includes:

> First-aid kit
> Water
> Insect repellent
> Sunscreen
> Topographic map and/or this book
> Road map
> Folding saw for removing small windfalls
> Rain clothes
> Hat
> Sunglasses
> Bandana
> Extra paddle

By Massachusetts law, canoeists must wear Coast Guard-approved personal flotation devices between September 15 and May 15. Nonswimmers and weak swimmers should always wear them. One approved personal flotation device must be in the boat for each person at all times.

If there will be portages, wear long pants for protection from poison ivy, thorns, and mosquitoes. Long pants also prevent the vicious top-of-the-thighs sunburns that can afflict canoeists in shorts.

Where to Go

The trip will begin and end with an access point, which is a place where cars can be parked and canoes can be put into the water. On the maps, canoe access points are shown with a dot and labelled with a number that refers to the description in the text. Places where riverside walks can begin but canoes cannot be launched are labelled with capital letters.

Most canoeists want the river's current behind them, so they plan to paddle downstream. Only on short trips is it practical to return to the starting point by canoe. This means that two cars are involved in many canoe outings. After one car has been "spotted" at the downstream destination, the boats and people go to the upstream starting point, put in, and begin their journey. If only one car is available, it is possible to spot a bicycle downstream or to take a bicycle in the canoe.

Travel Time

How long it takes to cover a given stretch of river depends on the speed of the current, the wind, the strength of the paddlers, how often and how long they stop, and the portages if there are any. In general, you can birdwatch or fish and float along at about one mile per hour. Steadier nonathletic paddling covers about two miles per hour. Strong, steady paddling is faster but only those who regularly practice this sport should count on making higher speeds. Each access point is labelled with its "river mile," which is the distance downstream from the Echo Lake Dam. These are derived from river mileages used by the United States Army Corps of Engineers and the Massachusetts Department of Environmental Protection, with interpolations measured on USGS maps. To find the length of a proposed canoe trip, subtract the river mile of the starting point from the river mile of the end (assuming the trip is upstream to downstream).

Tributaries

Five tributaries of the Charles can be explored by canoe when the water is high enough. They are Mine Brook, Mill River, Stop River, Bogastow Brook, and Waban Brook. It is safer to canoe small streams from downstream to upstream so the current pushes the boat away from obstructions, because brooks have tight twists that create blind corners. For this reason and because the sources of small streams are far above their heads of navigation, distances on tributaries are given from the point the stream meets the Charles.

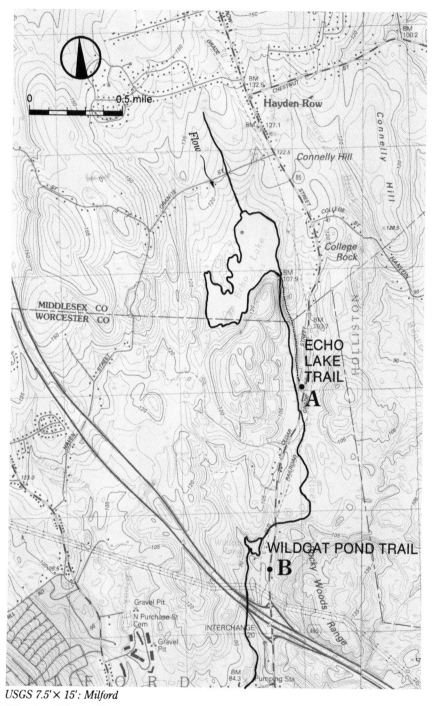

USGS 7.5' × 15': Milford

Charles River: Towns of Hopkinton, Milford

Headwaters

Access Points
Foot

A Echo Lake Trail, Milford and Hopkinton
NOTE: Because this is a source of supply for the
Milford Water Company, use of Echo Lake is restric-
ted. No boating is allowed. Permission to walk there
must be obtained from the Milford Water Company.
USGS Milford quadrangle
The trail, a dirt road to the base of the dam, intersects with Cedar Street (Route 85) near the
northern end of Milford. There is a pulloff at the
trailhead with parking for five cars.

B WILDCAT POND TRAIL, Milford
USGS Milford quadrangle
The Charles River meets its second dam at the out-
flow of Wildcat Pond a tenth of a mile west of Cedar
Street (Route 85). Two cars can be parked along the
dirt road to the pond.

Comments
For the purpose of expressing distances from its source,
the Charles River begins at the Echo Lake Dam. Three
tributary brooks flow into Echo Lake, carrying runoff
from the south side of Hopkinton's large central hill. One
of the brooks originates in a trickle high on the hill.
Because it is the highest tributary of the main stem of the
river this brook is considered the ultimate source of the
Charles River. But at its source a brook flows intermittently varying with the weather, so it is impossible to pin-
point where it begins. For this reason the Echo Lake Dam
is used as mile 0.0 of the Charles River.

In its natural condition Echo Lake was a swamp in
which the Charles paused and gathered before tumbling
down a narrow valley, a notch in the south side of the
granite basin. The Milford Water Company built the Echo
Lake Dam across the outlet. The dam is in Hopkinton, as
is most of the lake. A map dated 1831 shows Sheffield's
Sawmill where the dam is today, but the mill pond was
small. The dam must have been a low one.

When the Milford Water Company was formed in
1881, the upper watershed of the Charles was chosen as
the source of supply because it was a very sparsely populated area. The company built a twenty-two foot dam,
creating a lake of seventy-one acres and storage of 103
million gallons. The summer of 1900 was extremely dry,
and the company's reserve of water shrank uncomfortably
close to nothing. It was determined to increase the size of
the reservoir by raising the dam. Although there are
scant records of the construction of the original dam, the
improvements of 1902 are well documented and extensively photographed.

The old dam had spanned the valley from one bedrock
wall to the other but it had not reached ledge at the bottom of the gorge, a deficiency that was corrected in 1902.
The new dam was carefully bonded to the bedrock.
Blocks of granite were quarried on the site from outcrops
to the left of the dam and were swung into place by a
derrick. Guy lines supporting the derrick were attached
to the ledge with steel pins which are still in place.

The Milford Water Company's filters and pumps are
two and a half miles downstream of the dam. Until 1978
water flowed from the reservoir through its natural channel to the company's intakes at the plant on Dilla Street.
Because the above-ground water was too vulnerable to
contamination and too much water was taken up by
vegetation along the way, the company installed a twenty-
four inch pipe from Echo Lake to Dilla Street. The pipe
runs beneath the grade of the Hopkinton and Milford
Railroad. Only surplus water enters the above-ground
channel; the rest is supplied by the company to the
residents of Milford, Hopedale, and Mendon. Most of this
water is returned to the river at the south end of Milford
where the effluent of the Milford Waste Water Treatment
Facility enters the Charles.

The trail from the dam parallels the infant river as it
passes through a granite-walled valley. At mile 0.7 the
trail ends at the pulloff and the stream flows under Route
85. For the next three-quarters of a mile the Charles
curves through a swampy area east of the road, then

crosses under it again to enter Wildcat Pond. The land to the west of the road is drained by Deer Brook. It has striking granite ledges and abandoned quarries.

Deer Brook and the Charles flow through Wildcat Pond. There was a sawmill here in 1844. The Milford Water Company bought the property in 1885, and built a new dam in 1918. Although the area is posted, word from the Milford Water Company is that walkers do not need permission to visit here. Unfortunately, the beauty of the area is marred by illegal dumping.

At mile 2.0 the river is crossed by Boston Edison transmission lines. These high voltage lines (345 kilovolts) run west from a major substation in Medway to Millbury, where they fork to New York and to the James Bay hydroelectric plant in Canada.

There is no canoeing in this uppermost section of the Charles; boating is not permitted on Echo Lake, and the river-to-be is merely a slender brook.

Echo Lake, source of the Charles River, is a reservoir owned by the Milford Water Company.

Suggested Outings

Walks

— Walk to Echo Lake. Those charmed by the natural sculptures of ledge outcrops will enjoy visiting the terrain around the upper Charles, where Milford granite is at or near the surface. Due to problems with vandalism the Milford Water Company restricts use, but responsible walkers are welcome if they call the company in advance or stop by the office. The address is Milford Water Company, 42 B Dilla Street, Milford, Massachusetts, 01754-1154, telephone (508) 473-5110.

Distance: 1.4 miles round trip on the trail. The walk can be extended on the railroad grade or on other trails in the area.

Parking: Access A

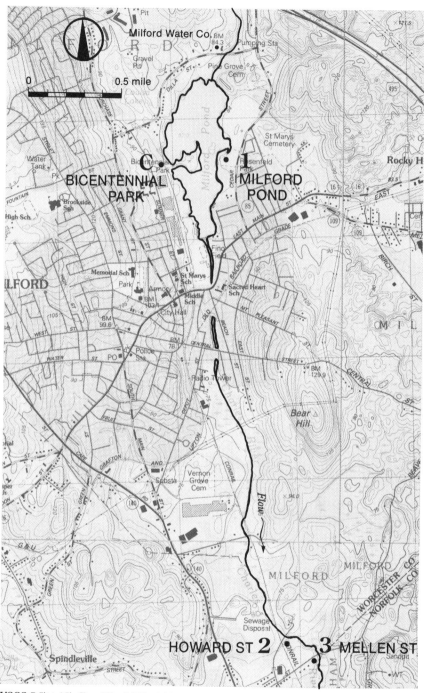

USGS 7.5' × 15': Franklin, Milford, Uxbridge

Charles River: Towns of Bellingham, Hopedale, Milford

Milford Pond

Access Points

Canoe

1 MILFORD POND (Cedar Swamp Pond), Milford (mile 2.8)
USGS Milford quadrangle
Rosenfeld Park is entered from Cedar Street (Route 85). The parking lot accomodates twenty or more cars. A dirt road at the rear of the parking lot leads to the edge of the pond. If the park's automobile gate is closed, three cars can be parked along the road.

2 HOWARD STREET, Hopedale (mile 5.7)
USGS Uxbridge quadrangle
In high water, canoeing can begin here. Four cars can be parked near the bridge.

3 MELLEN STREET, Hopedale and Bellingham (mile 5.9)
USGS Uxbridge quadrangle
Two cars can be parked near the bridge. It is easier to launch at Mellen Street, but the parking is better at Howard Street.

Foot

C BICENTENNIAL PARK, Milford
USGS Milford Quadrangle
The large peninsula projecting into Milford Pond can be reached from a parking lot on Sumner Street. A trail around the periphery of the peninsula affords a good view of the pond.

Comments

Below Route 495, the Charles enters the Milford Water Company's Dilla Street facility. The low dam at Dilla Street diverts water into the company's intakes. Four "slow sand filters" cleanse the water before it is pumped into the distribution mains. Water brought from the reservoir by pipe as well as water arriving through the above-ground channel enters the system. Water that passes over the dam at Dilla Street has almost, but not quite, escaped collection by the Milford Water Company, because at this point it enters Milford Pond. The company has a well deep beneath the pond's bottom that takes water seeping down from the pond.

Only new maps refer to this as Milford Pond. Old maps call it Cedar Swamp Pond, which invites confusion with the pond of that name that is the source of the Sudbury River, in Westborough, a few miles up Route 495.

Milford Pond can be visited on foot or by canoe. The pond is clogged with aquatic vegetation, including pickerelweed, pondweed, cattails, phragmites, and pond lilies. The heavy vegetation is the result of the pollution of recent decades; before the pollution this pond was popular for recreational boating. Insects and their predators persist, and

many waterfowl visit the pond. St. Mary of the Assumption Church, built in 1848 of Milford granite, rises from high ground to the south, its square tower visible throughout the pond. The dam is on East Main Street (Route 16), opposite the Sacred Heart Church, which has a pointed spire. Bear Hill is in the distance to the left of the church. The outlet of Milford Pond was the site of mills beginning in 1705. In 1794 there were grist and fulling mills here, and in 1854 a grist mill and a sawmill. Fulling was a process for finishing homemade wool cloth.

For two miles below Milford Pond the Charles is not canoeable. It enters a culvert that takes it beneath the street and buildings. It reappears briefly, confined to a stone-lined channel. At Central Street it ducks under the Archer Rubber Company, after which it enters an inaccessible wetland.

The Charles is subject to occasional pollution from Milford's combined-sewer overflows. This means that during periods of heavy rain some sewage enters the river. The town is taking steps to correct this situation.

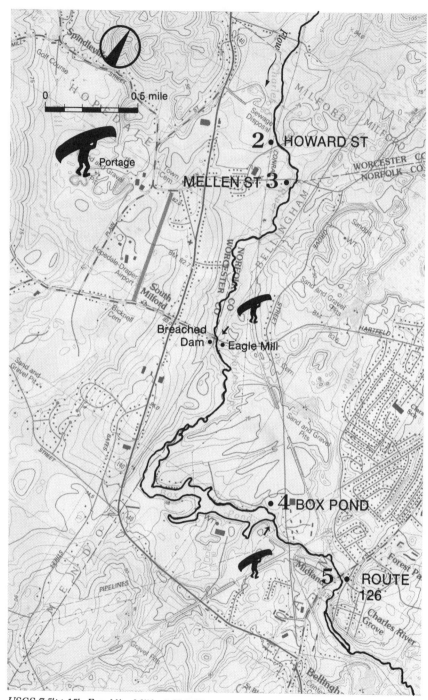

2 • HOWARD ST

MELLEN ST 3 •

Portage

Sewage
Disposal

Breached
Dam • • Eagle Mill

• 4 BOX POND

5 • ROUTE
126

USGS 7.5' × 15': *Franklin, Milford, Uxbridge*

Charles River: Towns of Bellingham, Hopedale, Mendon, Milford

Box Pond

Access Points

Canoe

2 HOWARD STREET, Hopedale (mile 5.7)
USGS Uxbridge quadrangle
In high water, canoeing can begin here. Four cars can
be parked near the bridge.

3 MELLEN STREET, Hopedale and Bellingham (mile
5.9)
USGS Uxbridge quadrangle
Two cars can be squeezed along the road. It is easier
to launch at Mellen Street, but the parking is better at
Howard Street.

4 BOX POND, Bellingham (mile 8.4)
USGS Franklin quadrangle
Box Pond Road bends where it meets the pond. Seven
cars can be parked in the pulloffs.

5 ROUTE 126 (North Main Street), Bellingham (mile
9.1)
USGS Franklin quadrangle
Parking for three cars and a good canoe launch are on
a side street, First Avenue, to the left of the river.

Comments
Those wishing to canoe the whole Charles River can begin
at Howard Street. Just upriver the Milford Waste Water
Treatment Facility restores to the Charles the water taken
at Echo Lake. The effluent from this plant contributes a
large percentage of the river at this point. Fortunately, the
effluent from this modern plant is above reproach. If this
water were diverted for other purposes the river's flow
would remain scanty for miles downstream.

At Howard Street the Charles borders a farm, and canoeists attract interest from the horses. The left bank is Milford; the right is Hopedale, the site of one of the experimental social communities of the reform era of the mid-1800s (see page 198). At Mellen Street Bellingham takes over the left bank. Below Mellen Street the river flows through a marsh of sedge and cattail. At points the channel is obstructed by willows and red maples.

The marsh above the Hartford Avenue Bridge has grown up from the bed of what was called Factory Pond. The dam that formed the pond was just below the bridge, at mile 6.9. Three towns meet at the bridge: Hopedale bounds Mendon on the right bank, and Bellingham is on the left. The nearby village is called South Milford, because Hopedale was part of Milford until 1868. The dam that impounded Factory Pond broke in 1919. The rapid drop that made this a logical mill site requires canoeists to negotiate a difficult portage on the left, next to the face of a sluiceway in the old dam. A woolen mill was built here in 1812. The remains of the three-story stone building stand, partially overgrown, next to a private residence, near the swimming pool. This was the Eagle Mill, which burned in 1868. Because there is neither parking nor launch site at Hartford Avenue, this is not an access point.

There are big white pines below the bridge on the right bank, which has the higher ground; the left bank is lower and has red maples. Here the river is wide enough for comfortable paddling, but it narrows entering the shrub swamp above Box Pond, where canoeists must struggle through shrubs and blown-down trees, and the trash they have collected. At some points shrubs growing on one side of the channel reach across and touch those on the other side.

Cottages line the shore of Box Pond. Where the pond bends to the left Mendon is left behind, and for the next five miles the Charles River is the exclusive possession of Bellingham. Access 3 is on the left shore of the pond, within sight of the dam, which is portaged on the right. There is a long history of saw and grist mills at Box Pond, and a woolen mill was built here in the 1930s. Below the dam the river flows through woods. To the right a gas-fired power plant is, at this writing, under construction.

At mile 8.7 is the Depot Street bridge, a single arch of stone blocks. The area at and around the bridge has accumulated trash such as tires, oil drums, and shopping carts. Without high water the flow is not sufficient to avoid these obstructions. There is a railroad bridge at mile 8.8. The mouth of Beaver Brook at mile 9.0 tempts exploration, but alders, silver maples, and shallow water soon bar upstream penetration. Access 5 is on the left, fifty yards downstream of the North Main Street (Route 126) bridge.

Although a run of this section of the river is possible, it should be undertaken only by determined and experienced canoeists. The convenient outings lie farther downstream.

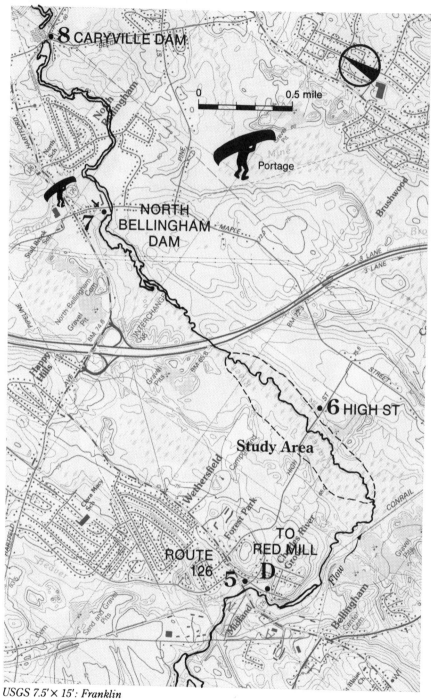

Charles River: Town of Bellingham

Bellingham Meadows

Access Points

Canoe

5 ROUTE 126 (North Main Street), Bellingham
(mile 9.1)
USGS Franklin quadrangle
Parking for three cars and a good canoe launch are on
a side street, First Avenue, to the left of the river.

6 HIGH STREET, Bellingham (mile 11.1)
USGS Franklin quadrangle
High Street bisects Bellingham Meadows, approaching
the river from both banks on causeways that are too
narrow for ideal parking, but three cars can be
squeezed off the road at the bridge approaches.

7 NORTH BELLINGHAM DAM, Bellingham (mile 12.9)
USGS Bellingham quadrangle
On the river's left a dirt road leads from the upstream
side of Maple Street fifty yards into the trees to a
parking area large enough for four cars. Upstream and
downstream launches are reached from there.

8 CARYVILLE DAM, Bellingham (mile 13.9)
USGS Medfield quadrangle
The upstream canoe launch is off Pearl Street on the
river's right, where four cars can be parked along the
river. Canoeists headed downstream put in behind the
mill buildings. The right side is better if the gate is
open and access is permitted.

Foot

D Trail to site of RED MILL, Bellingham
USGS Franklin Quadrangle
Four cars can be parked along First Avenue opposite
the entrance to the trail that parallels the emptied mill
pond.

Comments

Below North Main Street the river zigzags through woods. A riffle is reached at mile 9.6, where the river shoots through the breach in an old dam. An 1852 photograph of this location shows no trees or shrubs on either river bank, and a neat one-story frame mill building standing at the left end of the dam. It was called the Red Mill. The railroad ran along the right bank in 1852, as it does today. This area, called Charles River Grove, lies on the southernmost bend in the Charles. It is forty-two degrees and five minutes north of the equator. The most northerly point is at the Moody Street Dam in Waltham, where the Charles is a third of a degree nearer the north pole.

The shrub swamp below Charles River Grove does not offer much of a channel, and what channel there is is obstructed at some points by trash. Passage is possible in high water. The stream has more definition in the marsh below the shrub swamp. This big meadow gives the section its name and is discussed below as a study area. Wrentham's farmers cut hay in the meadow long before anyone ventured to settle in Bellingham; it was too isolated. Access 6 is at High Street, which bisects the meadow at mile 11.1.

Route 495 is at river mile 11.9, its bridge dated 1965. Three concrete tunnels carry the Charles beneath the highway. At high water there is not enough room for a canoe between the water and the concrete ceiling, which is lower at the downstream end than at its upstream entrance. Because portaging is discouraged by chain-link fences and heavy traffic, downstream passage is impossible for some of the year. It is not by oversight that the Route 495 culverts have little headroom. They are designed to limit the flow. In the 1950s, hurricanes Carol and Diane caused flooding in Boston. The Route 495 bridge does double duty: it takes traffic across the river, and it restricts the rate at which floodwater from the upper Charles can descend. It is, in effect, a flood control structure.

Below Route 495, a channel five feet wide winds between grassy banks. The pond of the North Bellingham Dam is sinuous and not without some current. Above the dam the takeout is on the left, at Access 7. The portage passes through the small parking area and follows a faint path down to the river.

At Maple Street is the village of North Bellingham,

where a cotton mill was built in 1810. For details of the history of this and the other Bellingham mills, see page 195. The three-story stone mill building is marked 1880; its windows are boarded up, but other sections of the mill complex remain in use. It would be easy to launch a canoe from the parking lot, but it has been posted against trespassing and enforcement is vigorous.

Just below the Maple Street Bridge is a ledge and a considerable drop in the river. Fallen trees barricade the narrow stream unless they are removed by local canoeists. Downstream from the ledge begins a smooth run in quickwater. The mouth of Stall Brook is passed at mile 13.1. Red maple, jewelweed, and wild grape grow along the shady banks. Where there is more sun the dominant riverside shrub is kinnikinnick, a wetland dogwood pictured on page 93. Arrowwood, burreed, royal fern, and grape are beside kinnikinnick, and in mid-July the pink flowers of swamp rose add color to the lush green riverbanks. There is much aquatic vegetation: pondweed, coontail, and elodea. The natural beauty is blemished by the presence of manmade trash.

The bridge of a subdivision street called Plymouth Road is at mile 13.5.

A short distance above Caryville, where the Charles takes a sharp turn to the right, there is a stand of tupelo trees. Tupelo, also called sour gum or black gum, has shiny green leaves. Its scientific name is *Nyssa sylvatica,* and it grows in moist soil.

Siltation and the lush growth of marsh plants have diminished the Caryville millpond. Wild rice, which flowers in August and produces nutricious food for wildlife, is abundant in the pond. It is possible to land canoes above the dam on either side, but the right is preferable.

Suggested Outings

Canoe

— The Bellingham Meadows study area is worth a visit. Paddle upstream first to test yourself against the current, which can be fairly stiff.
Distance: Variable. A round trip of 2.5 miles includes paddling up beyond High Street to the shrub swamp, descending to Route 495, then returning to the start.
Portages: None
Parking: Access 6

— Explore upstream from Caryville.
Distance: Variable. A round trip of up to 2.4 miles is
possible.
Portages: None
Parking: Access 8

Bellingham Meadows Study Area
One of the good things that has happened to the Charles
River is the Natural Valley Storage Project. Charged with
controlling flooding on the Charles River, the New
England Division of the Army Corps of Engineers proposed the construction of a new dam at the river's mouth,
and the preservation of wetlands along the valley. The
new dam has pumps capable of ejecting water from the
Basin even if the water level in the harbor is above that of
the Basin. Powerful though these pumps are, there is a
limit to their capacity. The purpose of the Natural Valley
Storage Project, which Congress approved in 1974, is to
slow the progress of Boston-bound floodwater by protect-
ing the ability of the meadows to absorb much of the
excess. The marsh in Bellingham is preserved along with
7800 other wetland acres so that Boston's Storrow Drive
can always be travelled by car and never by boat. (See
map on page 208.)

The Corps of Engineers refers to each of the Natural
Valley Storage Project's seventeen wetlands by a letter of
the alphabet. Bellingham Meadows is Area S. The Corps
of Engineers plans recreational use in accordance with
objectives that include conservation of ecological resources. The Corps' 1984 Master Plan for Recreation Resources Development says:

> Area S is located on the Charles River in
> Bellingham.This is the first significant wetland encoun-
> tered along the Charles downstream of Cedar Swamp
> Pond [Milford Pond] in Milford. The river channel
> reflects a sudden change in gradient by assuming a
> meandering character after leaving a relatively straight
> channel at Charles River Grove. The river edge is a
> wet meadow which gradually changes to shrub swamp
> and woodland. At the downstream or northern end of
> this wetland, the river channel widens into the pool of
> North Bellingham Dam.

> Fee acreage in Area S totals 330 acres in an almost
> continuous block along two linear miles of the Charles.
> Interstate 495 bisects the project area. Public access is
> only available from High Street in Bellingham, with
> parking limited to the road shoulders.

The phrase "fee acreage" refers to land that the Corps of Engineers purchased outright, distinguished from land for which the Corps bought "flowage easements" that prohibit encroachment.

The Corps of Engineers permits canoeing on the waters of the Natural Valley Storage Project areas. Management has been leased to the Massachusetts Division of Fisheries and Wildlife, which has erected signs, and which stocks fish in suitable habitats.

Water absorbed by wetlands is slowly released to the river, which helps maintain stream levels during dry periods. By filtering impurities, the marsh cleanses water that recharges underground water supplies. Plants such as cattails, which are numerous in Bellingham Meadows, remove excess nutrients from the river water. The middle of the Charles is relatively clean because pollution from Milford's combined sewer overflows is removed by the vegetation.

Cattails offer room and board to many invertebrates. The air force of insects is more visible after sunset, seen then against a faded sky. The big dragonflies called darners cruise low. On patrol in the twilight, they feed freely on the smaller, weaker insects that flutter up from the marsh plants. Mosquitoes are feeble fliers, easily plucked from the air by the masterful dragonflies. Darners' heads glisten with eyes that cover them like a helmet. Their

thoraxes bulge with flight muscles capable of producing 1600 beats per minute of wings spanning five inches. They have been perfecting their flight skills generation after generation for about 200 million years.

Red-eyed vireo

Songbirds such as red-eyed vireos rely on insects for their sustenance. The greatest variety of birds is seen in middle and late spring. A red-eyed vireo might greet a visitor at that season, singing from a perch over the High Street causeway, its song similar to the robin's. Red-eyed vireos sing all day and continue their song longer into the summer than most birds. Male vireos sing even while incubating the eggs. Rather drab in color, gray crowned, and olive backed, the red-eyed vireo is recognized by its vireo body shape, and by the long white stripe above its eyes, made the more vivid by a black line along its top. When the light is right, its eyes do look distinctly red.

Vegetation along the causeway includes gray birch, wild rose, swamp white oak, arrowwood, and red maple. Out on the meadows, cattails, wild rice, bulrushes, and purple loosestrife fringe the Charles. Shrubs include common elder and winterberry. Scattered black willows serve as song perches for willow flycatchers (they sing *fitz bew, fetzbew!*) and great crested flycatchers. The great crested flycatcher is similar to the eastern kingbird in size, posture, and some aspects of its behavior. They are both about nine inches long, but the great crested flycatcher has a longer bill and a much different color scheme. Eastern kingbirds are black and white, while great crested flycatchers wear earthy hues of brown, olive, and yellow. A spring visit to Bellingham Meadows might also yield sightings of cedar waxwings, warbling vireos, common grackles, red-winged blackbirds, and tree swallows.

Great crested flycatchers are part of the natural community at Bellingham Meadows.

27

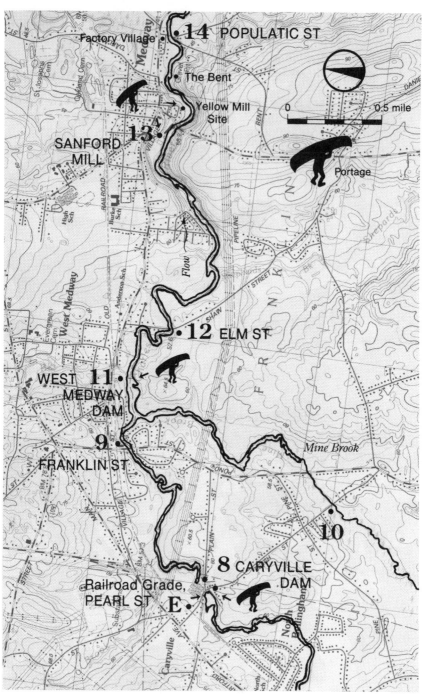

USGS 7.5′ × 15′: Franklin, Medfield

Charles River: Towns of Bellingham, Medway

The Mills of Medway

Access Points

Canoe

8 CARYVILLE DAM, Bellingham (mile 13.9)
   USGS Medfield quadrangle
   The Caryville mills are on Pearl Street. Canoeists
   headed downstream put in behind the mill buildings.
   The right side is nicer if the gate is open and access is
   permitted. Four cars can be parked along the river.

9 FRANKLIN STREET, Medway (mile 15.6)
   USGS Medfield quadrangle
   Canoes can be launched from the bank downstream to
   the left of the bridge. Five or more cars can be parked
   off the road near the river.

10 See "Mine Brook," page 37.

11 WEST MEDWAY DAM, Medway (mile 16.0)
   USGS Medfield quadrangle
   Five or more cars can be parked at the intersection of
   Village Street and Cottage Street. In high water
   canoes can be launched into Chicken Brook, which
   enters the river below the dam. To put in upstream
   from the dam, canoes must be carried about one hundred yards to the river.

12 ELM STREET, Franklin (mile 16.5)
   USGS Medfield quadrangle
   The launch is to the right of the bridge, on the
   upstream side. There is room for two cars along the
   road.

13 SANFORD MILL, Medway (mile 17.8)
   USGS Medfield quadrangle
   The Sanford Mill is on the left side at the high bridge.
   The street crossing the bridge is Sanford Street in

Medway and Lincoln Street in Franklin. The upstream launch is on the left bank, in the parking lot behind the mill buildings, which have been converted to condominiums. Most of the parking places are for residents, but space near the river is provided for canoeists.

To enter the rapid below the dam, cross the canal at the bend in River Street and carry across the island. Two cars will fit along River Street.

14 POPULATIC STREET (Walker Street), Medway (mile 18.4)
USGS Medfield quadrangle
The launch is on the river's right, upstream of the Red Bridge. Six cars can be left in parking areas on each side of the bridge.

Foot

E OLD RAILROAD GRADE at PEARL STREET, Bellingham
USGS Medfield quadrangle
Four cars can be parked on Pearl Street near its intersection with the trail, which is adjacent to a vacant lot with a large beech tree.

Comments

Caryville is the most downstream of Bellingham's mill sites. The river falls about fifty feet in Bellingham, mostly at dams. The Charles drops another fifty feet while passing between Medway and Franklin, then descends slowly to South Natick. The tall brick chimney at Caryville says "1899." The chimney is a reminder that steam power supplemented water power at Massachusetts textile mills.

After spilling over Caryville Dam the Charles flows beneath the mill building and emerges between concrete walls. Canoes can be launched from either bank just below these walls if the property owners continue to allow access. If continuing a downstream journey, portage around the dam and the mill. A portage on the right is 215 yards. If the gate is closed and it is necessary to go to the left the distance is about 375 yards.

Not far downstream, piles of stones (apparently placed by neighborhood children) obstruct the current at low water. A number of cultural artifacts are in and along the river here: a refrigerator, clothes dryer, shopping cart, hot-water heater, and automobile wheels. Plain Street runs near the river's right, and has been used for dumping.

In the shade of the deep woods, sweet pepperbush opens its flowers in late July. In some places vines of poison ivy hang from limbs near the bank. The shade is interrupted at the power lines (mile 14.2), and here the banks are lined with sun-loving plants: sensitive fern, purple loosestrife, tall meadow rue, and honeysuckle, which by midsummer has red berries in pairs.

The woods resume below the transmission lines. There is a stand of sassafras on the left bank, interspersed with greenbrier and winterberry. The riverbank is accessible on foot here, reached from the old railroad bed on the river's left. The mouth of Hopping Brook is at mile 14.7 on the left. At this point Medway replaces Bellingham as the town on the left. Hopping Brook drains western Medway and Holliston, and a little of Ashland. Its water is clear with a yellowish tint; its bed is gravel and sand. Below Hopping Brook the river has a brisk current, but it passes silently over the smooth sandy bottom. The banks are well-defined, wooded and undeveloped. The trees include red maple, ash, and shagbark hickory. It is lovely to canoe this half-mile reach.

Where the river's gradient flattens a bit, the banks become swampier. The channel splits; canoeists should bear right. The banks are lined with jewelweed, kinnikinnick, sensitive fern, purple loosestrife, and buttonbush. In the water are pondweed and elodea. By mid-summer, as the buttonbush and jewelweed begin to flower, the blackbirds are no longer dispersed for nesting and are seen in flocks.

The river enters a residential area as it begins to slacken behind the West Medway Dam. The bridge at mile 15.6 joins Medway on the left to Franklin on the right. The street is Franklin Street in Medway, and Pond Street in Franklin. Access 9 is on the left bank below the bridge. Trout are sometimes taken from this section of the Charles, as well as large-mouthed bass and pickerel.

The mouth of Mine Brook (river mile 15.8) is broad because it is part of the West Medway impoundment. Mine Brook is described in a separate section beginning on page 37.

The West Medway Dam is reached at mile 16.0. It is not very convenient to reach the Access 11 parking area from this dam. Medway's Village Street is about a hundred yards to the left of the river.

The West Medway Dam is portaged on the right. The mill foundation is on the left.

The first dam at this site was constructed about 1812. Of the series of industries carried on at West Medway, paper making predominated. The Campbell Paper Mill began operations in 1854. By the time it burned in the 1890s it was Greenwood's Paper Factory. Greenwood also ran a paper mill downstream at "Baltimore," in Millis where Route 115 crosses the Charles.

The first bridge below the dam serves a private residence, that of Mrs. Thelma Cherry, who has lived here since 1956. Mrs. Cherry recalls several drownings at the West Medway Dam, and warns, "The river becomes very formidable in the spring." Though Mrs. Cherry's home is in Franklin, her driveway crosses the river to Medway. Her bridge is made of telephone poles set on concrete abutments. In the late 1800s this was Woodland Park, owned by George Henry Parker, who created a small zoo, a baseball diamond (Medway's first baseball club was formed in 1851), a dancehall, a theater, and a boathouse. Special street cars came here on weekends.

Its flow has been swollen with Hopping, Mine, and Chicken Brooks, and now the Charles has gained the stature of a

The White Mill, built in 1812, was later demolished and replaced by the brick Sanford Mill. In 1846, a stone bridge was constructed near the mill, joining Medway and Franklin.

river. Red maples reach from both banks to form an arching
canopy above the stream. At the meanders above Elm
Street is common elder, *Sambucus canadensis*. Its
fragrant white flowers appear in early June. Also present
is another common riverside shrub, arrowwood, which
blossoms as the elder goes by.

The Charles passes briskly under the stone arch of
the Elm Street-Shaw Street bridge at mile 16.5. Access 12
is on the right, upstream of the bridge. The steep sandy
bank beyond the bridge has a nice mixture of wildflowers,
including swamp azalea, which is pictured on page 93.

After paralleling Elm Street and the power lines and
passing the mouth of Shepherds Brook, the Charles
curves to the left and enters a steep-sided valley. The
river has a unique beauty during its mile-long passage
through this valley. The right bank is particularly steep
and is covered with mature hemlocks. At the bend that
brings the canoeist in sight of the Sanford Mill there is a
large boulder, the "Big Rock," which was a famous
swimming spot for generations of Medway's children.

The Medway Dam is at mile 17.8 beside the brick
Sanford Mill. In 1711, Deacon John Whiting had a grist
mill at "The Narrows," which is now the Medway Dam.
There was no bridge except for a walkway along the top
of the dam. The first bridge was built in 1806. Whiting
operated a mill from 1711 to 1805, when Philo Sanford
inherited it and formed the Medway Cotton Manufactory.
Sanford's was the third commercial cotton mill in the
United States, after those at Pawtucket and Beverly. Sanford hired a mechanic who had managed a mill at Pawtucket, luring him away with a house, ten cords of wood per
year, and $2.00 per day. Sanford's "White Mill" was built
in 1812 and operated until 1883, when it was replaced
with the four-story brick mill that still stands. The concrete dam was built around 1929.

In 1739 Medway and Wrentham built a bridge here. It
was declared unsafe in 1844. A stone-arch bridge was
built in 1846, but it collapsed immediately after the
dedication ceremony. The replacement was finished in
1847. In 1911 the stone arch at the center was replaced
with one of concrete, but the masonry walls dating from
1847 still support the approaches and are visible from
downstream.

Canoes can be landed on the left bank above the mill

building (Access 13). The portage is around the mill, across Sanford Street, down River Street to the place where it turns sharply, across the old canal and finally to the river on the other side of the island. The distance is about 500 yards. There is poison ivy on the island at the downstream end of the portage.

Below the dam the Charles has a brief spell of white water. Class I rapids tumble several hundred yards below the Medway dam. In high water there is excitement here; otherwise it is too rocky to canoe. It is possible to continue the portage along the island on left bank, skirting almost all of the fast water.

This island was the site of William H. Cary's Yellow Mill, which was built in 1837 and burned in 1854. After the fire Cary moved upriver to Bellingham, to the village that became Caryville, where he built with brick and stone. By 1884 Eaton and Wilson Company had a large mill on the island that produced cotton wadding for use as padding and in cartridges. The long, narrow structure had a carding room at its upstream end, a drying room spanning the water wheel, and a finishing room at the downstream end. Waterpower was supplemented by an eighty-horsepower steam boiler. A ninety-foot chimney rose beside the boiler. Across the canal, at the bend in River Street, was a store house.

Water was diverted into the upper canal by a low dam one-tenth of a mile below the Sanford Street bridge. The canal supplied water to the big wheel in the center of the mill. Winter visitors to the island can easily discern the wheel pit and the foundations of the long building and power plant. A lower canal served as a tail-race, to return water to the river. In the summer much of this is obscured by poison ivy, which does well in places that have shade and moist soil, especially if the orginal vegetation has been disturbed by human activities.

Throughout the nineteenth century the Charles was lined with mills from Sanford Street to Populatic Street. Before the revolutionary war Ichabod Haws had a sawmill, a forge with a trip hammer, and a machine for boring gun barrels at "the Bent" at the foot of Oakland Street. In 1812 the Bent had three mills. Canals were built to distribute the water. There were two large tenements to house workers. The lowest of the Medway mills was at "Factory Village," at the Populatic Street Bridge. A bleachery was started here around 1821. There was a sawmill on the right bank and a series of industries on the left in 1884, and a decade later a dam above the bridge was still supplying water to the canal that paralleled Canal Street. The Eaton and Wilson Company made cotton batting (used in quilts) at a mill on the left bank below the bridge. An old building that was part of a shoddy mill still stands on the right bank.

The Populatic Street Bridge (mile 18.4) is also called the Red Bridge and is maintained in its traditional color.

Suggested Outings

Canoe

— Paddle upstream from the Sanford Mill and return to start.
Distance: Variable
Portages: None
Parking: Access 13 (Upstream launch site at mill building)

Walks

—The abandoned grade of the New York, New Haven and Hartford Railroad affords a stroll along the bank of the upper Charles. From Access E it runs in both directions perpendicular to Pearl Street. Heading upstream (southwest) the grade is clear for one-third of a mile before it ends at a backyard. The path is wide and level, shaded by oaks, about twenty feet above the river. Downstream, one-half mile is open, and there are nice paths that branch along the river's left bank, both above and below the mouth of Hopping Brook.
Parking: Access E

— Explore the site of the Eaton and Wilson Wadding Mill. This outing is best done in late fall, when deciduous plants have dropped their leaves, and at a time when the river is low or medium. Use stepping stones to cross the canal at the bend in River Street. The mill's foundations are on the left, spanning the wheel pit. Follow the dike along the canal upstream to the remains of the dam that supplied the canal. Farther upstream is a nice view of the high bridge and the dam.
Parking: Access 13, downstream

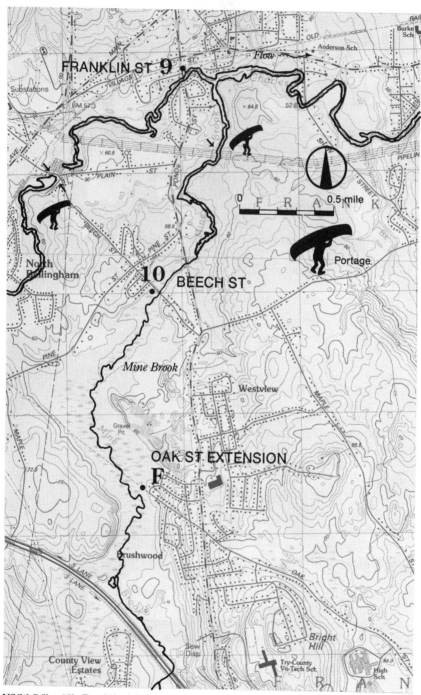

USGS 7.5′ × 15′: *Franklin, Medfield*

Mine Brook/Charles River: Towns of Franklin, Medway

Tributary
Mine Brook

Access Points

Canoe

9 FRANKLIN STREET, Medway (mile 5.6)
USGS Medfield quadrangle
Canoes can be launched from the bank downstream to
the left of the bridge. Five or more cars can be parked
off the road near the river.

10 BEECH STREET, Franklin
USGS Franklin quadrangle
Beech Street crosses Mine Brook 1.5 miles above the
Charles. Four cars can be parked along the road. The
launch is on the right, on the upstream side of the
bridge.

Foot

F Oak Street Extension, Franklin
USGS Franklin quadrangle
This road once crossed Mine Brook. The bridge was
reached by a quarter-mile causeway. The bridge is
gone, but the causeway allows pedestrians to visit the
shrub swamp. Three cars can be parked at the end of
Oak Street Extension.

Comments

The mouth of Mine Brook is one-fifth of a mile downstream
from Access 9 at Franklin Street. The lowest section of the
brook is backed up by the West Medway Dam. There is
good fishing where the brook enters the mill pond.

A rapid is reached at the crossing of the power lines, 0.4
miles upstream. It can be portaged on the brook's left.
Above the power lines is a small breached dam that can be
run in high water.

At the Franklin Country Day Camp a short, shallow
rapid requires a portage. Take out on the brook's right,
carry across the footbridge, and put in upstream on the
brook's left. Above the day camp, Mine Brook flows rapidly

over a boulder-strewn bed. A concrete dam forms a small pond. Upstream of the pond, a stone wall runs alongside the brook. At the Pond Street Bridge, the channel is shallow and rocky. There is no safe parking here.

The bridge at Beech Street is a concrete arch lined with a corrugated metal tube. Above Beech Street the streamsides are unlittered, but it is not easy to locate the channel. This splendid marsh, dominated by tussock sedge, is Area M of the Natural Valley Storage Project, containing 388 acres and extending along both sides of the brook beyond the head of canoe navigation. How many red-winged blackbirds make their homes in Area M and have the Corps of Engineers for their landlord? A visit in early May encountered many red-wings, plus hawks, crows, gray catbirds, a great blue heron, a sandpiper, and a yellow-rumped warbler. A muskrat was seen, and a 12″ pickerel was tempted from its lair beneath a buttonbush. The water plants were pondweed, elodea, and pickerel weed. Shrubs included wild rose and high-bush blueberry.

Those who persist in tracking the stream channel through several puzzling mazes of vegetation will eventually be turned back by the diffusion of the channel through impenetrable shrubs. The head of navigation is three miles above Mine Brook's mouth, and about one mile below Route 495. The causeways of old Oak Street extend into this shrub swamp.

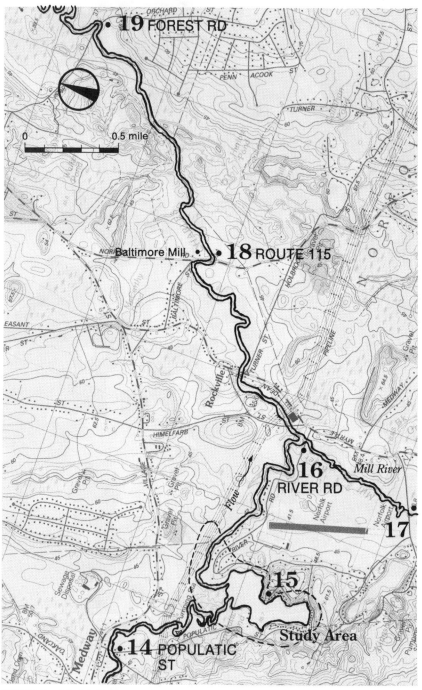

USGS 7.5' × 15': Medfield

Charles River: Towns of Franklin, Medway, Millis, Norfolk

Populatic
Pond

Access Points

Canoe

14 POPULATIC STREET (Walker Street), Medway
(mile 18.4)
USGS Medfield quadrangle
The launch is on the river's right, upstream of the
bridge. Six cars can be left in parking areas on each
side of the bridge.

15 POPULATIC POND, Norfolk (mile 19.9)
USGS Medfield quadrangle
There is a concrete boat ramp at the intersection of
Priscilla Avenue and Lakeshore Drive. Six or more
cars can be parked along the road.

16 RIVER ROAD, Norfolk (mile 20.6)
USGS Medfield quadrangle
River road crosses the Mill River at its junction with
the Charles. Four cars can be parked in pulloffs, and
additional parking can be improvised along the road.

17 See Mill River, page 49.

18 ROUTE 115 (Baltimore Street), Millis and Norfolk
(mile 22.9)
USGS Medfield quadrangle
A maximum of three cars fit into the pulloff near the
launch, which is on the right downstream side of the
bridge. Canoes should be paddled upstream under the
bridge into the slack water, then across to the left side
of the river. Below the bridge, the channel is on the
left; the right side is very shallow.

19 FOREST ROAD, Millis (mile 24.4)
USGS Medfield quadrangle
Six cars can be parked in a pulloff to the right of the
bridge. One canoe launch is on the upstream right side
of the bridge. A good alternative launch is 100 yards to

the east, on the downstream side. Four cars can be parked along the road in this area.

Comments

The terminal depot of the Medway Branch of the Norfolk County Railroad was near the right end of the Populatic Street bridge. This little railroad operated from 1853 to 1864 (see page 192). Trains crossed the river one-fifth of a mile downstream, where the power lines are now, and again just above Rockville before joining the main line at North Wrentham, which is now Norfolk. The bridge abutments are still visible.

As the Charles nears Populatic Pond, it winds through a marshy area in which abandoned river channels form fertile sloughs. The east and south shores and all of the water of Populatic Pond is in Norfolk, but the west bank is in Franklin, and the marsh separating the inlet from the outlet is in Medway. Canoeists arriving at Populatic Pond from upriver emerge into its northwest corner. To continue downstream turn left and follow the bank past 200 yards of swamp loosestrife to the stubby black willow marking the outflow channel.

Access 15 is an excellent launch site on the pond's east bank, a boat ramp at the intersection of Priscilla Avenue and Lakeshore Drive. Access 15 is across the northern lobe of the pond from the inlet and the outlet.

The mile-long outlet arm is a narrow extension of the pond itself, deeper than the main body of the pond. The channel is wide and there is little current. The "dam" is natural; it is bedrock near Myrtle Street. The houses on the right bank front on River Road. Kinnikinnick dominates the left bank. The modern wastewater treatment facility of the Charles River Pollution Control District, which serves the towns of Franklin, Medway, and Millis, discharges its effluent from a pipe at the bottom of the pond's outlet arm.

The mouth of a tributary called Mill River and Access 16 are reached at mile 20.6. The section on Mill River is on page 49.

As the river bends to the left, Myrtle Street comes into view. A sign on the Captain Joshua Partridge House indicates that it is location #24 on the Millis historical trail. Captain Partridge was the first commander of the Minutemen from this area. The house was built in 1734 at the site of an old Indian trading post where a ford provided easy crossing. The oldest roads followed the natives' trails, which crossed streams in shallow places where the bottom was firm. This is the case where the stream gradient is steep enough for the moving water to carry away the fine particles that form mucky bottoms.

There is shallow quickwater between Myrtle Street and the power lines. The abutments of the Medway Branch Railroad bridge are visible next to the power lines. A house occupies the railroad grade on the left bank. For the next two miles both banks are in Millis.

Large boulders scattered in the river announce the canoeist's approach to a village called Rockville. A cotton mill was built here in 1818. There is an island at the center of the span of the old shattered dam. At high water canoeists can pass to the left of the island. Be careful! This is a tricky spot. At medium water, the right channel is preferable. In low water, canoes must be carried over the island. It is best to avoid this part of the river when the river is low. At such times it is better to start canoeing at Access 19 or below.

Shallows continue intermittently below the bridge. A farm occupies the right bank for the last half mile above Baltimore Street (Route 115). Access 18 is at this bridge. This was called Jones' Bridge; at the time of the Civil War there was a paper mill on the left bank. The water is quite shallow below the bridge; the channel is on the left.

Below Baltimore Street canoeists enter a stunning stretch of river. For a mile and a half of easy paddling, the steady gentle stream pushes northeast between wooded hillsides. At mile 23.3, the mouth of an unnamed brook enters from the right. Below the brook, Norfolk is on the right bank, and Millis only on the left. The right bank has been posted ("Licensed Shooting Preserve") by a sportsman's club. On the left bank is a big woods, privately owned and unavailable for hiking. The Metropolitan District Commission's 1986 Charles River Corridor Plan gives this area the highest priority for protection.

The brook at mile 23.6 drains a chain of ponds. From the mouth of this brook a high ridge is visible ahead. This long, narrow formation extends along the river to the right, crossing the town boundary, as does the river, a tenth of a mile downstream. Medfield is now to the right of the Charles, the parent town of Medway and Millis, itself the offspring of Dedham.

With the exception of one modern house, the works of humanity are absent from this idyllic passage.

Approaching Forest Road there is a row of swamp white oaks on the left bank, then red maples, then pines, then the rip-rap bank of the causeway. The concrete bridge was built in 1984. One landing is on the right above the bridge. To reach the alternate landing, pass under the bridge (the abutments bear rather artistic graffiti), continue a tenth of a mile downstream, and land on the left.

Suggested Outings

Canoe

— A downstream run of this section is recommended for experienced canoeists.
Distance: 6 miles
Portages: In low water, one at Rockville
Parking:
    Upstream — Access 14
    Downstream — Access 19

— Paddle upstream between Millis and Norfolk. Start at Forest Road, go to the shallows below Baltimore Street, then return to start.
Distance: 3.0 miles round trip
Portages: None
Parking: Access 19

— Explore Populatic Pond
Distance: Variable
Portages: None
Parking: Access 15

Populatic Pond Study Area

Populatic Pond bears its Indian name, which means "Place to Fish." Before the Charles was dammed, herring spawned here, and Indians netted them in nearby brooks. Today's technology-oriented fishermen use bass boats equipped with sonar devices that indicate the depth of the water, the contour and probable texture of the bottom, and the size and location of fish. A tour of Populatic Pond in such a craft showed that, contrary to what one would guess from the dramatic steepness of its banks, Populatic Pond is shallow and its bottom is quite flat.

Populatic is a natural pond formed by the last glacier. About 15,000 years ago the ice sheet retreated, and the Charles River was born. Though rivers flowed over Massachusetts prior to glaciation, the great land-moving effects of the ice substantially altered drainage patterns. The river we know as the Charles is the product of post-glacial topography.

The ice withdrew, haltingly, from south to north. Populatic was the scene of one of the halts, a place where for many years the glacier neither retreated nor advanced. The southward flow of the ice was balanced by the annual meltoff. A tongue of ice projected south into the site of the future pond. To the east, a larger parallel lobe filled the valley of the Mill River. Year after year the glacier melted at the ends and sides of these lobes, and year after year the sand and gravel that had been frozen into the glacier was deposited around them. When the last ice melted, steep slopes were left to show where sand had piled up against a wall of ice. One of the steepest slopes at Populatic is beside the Access 15 boat ramp. The roots of the hemlocks hold the sandy soil in place.

Between the small tongue of ice that became Populatic and the larger lobe that became Mill River a flat sandy area formed upon which the Norfolk airport has been built. Because such flat places are accumulations carried from glaciers by meltwater, geologists call them "outwash plains."

Apparently the Charles River once flowed a quarter of a mile to the north of Populatic Pond, which was much deeper then. The young river side-slipped to the south and fell into the pond. Numerous channels were carved as the river moved; their ghosts are visible as eyebrow-shaped pools to the north of Populatic Pond, and as back-waters along the inflow channel. When the river entered Populatic, it began to deposit sand on the bottom of the pond. All ponds are temporary; the natural accretion of mineral and vegetable material eventually fills them. But this takes a long time, and some of eastern Massachusetts' "ice-block lakes" are still deep, cold, and clear. Walden Pond, for example, is 150 feet deep. At present, the main body of Populatic Pond has only two to seven feet of water. But the outflow channel is deeper, up to sixteen feet.

Why is the outflow channel so much deeper than the rest of the pond? When pieces of rock and mineral find themselves in flowing water, geologists call them sediments. Sediments are distinguished by size: they are boulders, cobbles, pebbles, sand, silt, and clay. Water moves sediments by rolling them along the bottom or by suspending them within the current. Sediments being moved by flowing water are called the "load" of the stream. Particles can be suspended in the current if the upward push of the turbulence within the water overcomes the pull of gravity that causes settling. Big rocks settle faster than small ones, other factors being equal. Pebbles settle faster than sand, and sand settles faster than silt. Flowing water needs to have more turbulent energy to suspend coarse sediments than fine ones.

Small cobbles, pebbles, and sand are usually pushed along the bottom, though in floods sand can be suspended. Particles in the bed load bump into each other. The abrasion resulting from these collisions turns rough chunks of rock into the rounded pebbles we associate with streambeds.

The capacity of a river to move sediment is determined largely by its gradient, which is the slope of the river as it tilts from its upland sources to the sea. River gradients are expressed in feet of vertical fall per mile of horizontal flow. The descent of the Charles averages four feet per mile, which means its profile is rather flat and its waters gentle. Mountain streams cascade eighty or more feet per mile.

The Charles River enters Populatic Pond carrying a load of sediment, having travelled miles through sandy country. In the pond the river's current dissipates. As the velocity of the water falls, particles drop from suspension. Year after year the pond has gradually filled. Approximately the same amount of water flows out of the pond as entered it, but most of the sediment load settled in the pond. The outflow current has the capacity to transport sediments, so it erodes the outflow channel. This is why Populatic's outflow is deeper than the rest of the pond.

When water is low in the Charles it is also low in Populatic Pond. When revealed by a dry spell, the margin of the pond is as clean as beach sand and firm enough to walk on in dress shoes. There is little vegetation in the pond, and without plants the food chain lacks a foundation, therefore Populatic has a sterility unusual for the Charles.

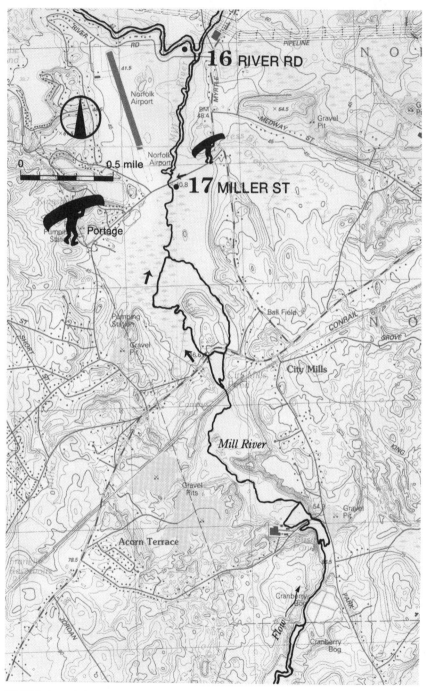

16 RIVER RD

Norfolk
Airport

0.5 mile

Portage

17 MILLER ST

City Mills

Mill River

Acorn Terrace

USGS 7.5' × 15': Franklin

Mill River/Charles River: Towns of Norfolk, Wrentham

Mill River

Access Points

Canoe

16 RIVER ROAD, Norfolk (mile 20.6)
   USGS Medfield quadrangle
   At its junction with the Charles, Mill River passes
   beneath River Road. Four cars can be parked in
   pulloffs, and additional parking can be improvised
   along the road.

17 MILLER STREET, Norfolk
   USGS Wrentham quadrangle
   Miller Street crosses Mill River 0.8 above the
   Charles. When there is enough water in the stream
   to canoe, there is no possibility of floating under this
   bridge. Both the upstream and downstream
   launches are on the right. Six cars can be parked on
   the downstream side of the right approach to the
   bridge.

Comments

The discharge of Mill River is less than that of Mine
Brook or of Bogastow Brook. The designation of some
tributaries as "rivers" while others are called brooks is a
product of local usage; Mill River's name is probably a
tribute to its historic importance as Wrentham's major
source of water power. Mill River is a brook. In southeastern states it would be Mill Run; in the midwest, Mill
Creek.

   Mill River flows under River Road through a corrugated metal culvert. Canoes cannot reach the Charles
through this culvert because of the stones just beyond its
downstream end. Those wishing to explore Mill River
either put in upstream of the culvert, or, if they have paddled from elsewhere on the Charles, make a quick portage over the road.

A purple-stemmed aquatic plant called water milfoil is conspicuous in Mill River. Smartweed and pickerelweed grow at the channel's edge, and purple loosestrife along the banks. A unique characteristic of this tributary is the dead maples that are found beside it, none of which is of large diameter. A sequence of events can be inferred. The water table in the streamside meadows must have declined enough in the past to permit the encroachment of trees. The event that caused this was probably the breaching of the Rockville Dam. At a later date the water table rose again, killing the trees — even red maples can stand only so many months of flooding. Probably it was the construction of River Road and its culvert that increased the upstream water level.

Miller Street is 0.8 miles above the Charles. The bridge is a low one and must be portaged. Above Miller Street in midsummer the aquatic vegetation is so lush that in places it is difficult to paddle. Elodea, pondweed, and milfoil are in the channel. Along the sides are burreed, pickerelweed, bladderwort, and rice cutgrass. White water lilies adorn the backwaters. Belted kingfishers, wood ducks, and American black ducks frequent the area. Though densely vegetated, the channel is wide and little current resists upstream passage. The water is clear and without odor.

The plant community gradually changes on the way up the stream to cattails, sweet gale, meadowsweet, and steeplebush. In the high water of spring or after a summer rain, perseverant canoeists can leave the marsh and paddle into the woods. They should stay alert for overhanging vines of poison ivy. The head of navigation is near a little footbridge two miles above the Charles. From here the ruin of an old building at City Mills is visible. Canoeists might wish to land and inspect this industrial village named so optimistically. In the heyday of City Mills, Norfolk did not yet exist; it was not set off from Wrentham until 1870.

At the footbridge the channel is too narrow to turn most canoes; it may be necessary to travel backwards until a wide spot is reached.

Suggested Outings

Canoe
— Paddle up Mill River and back from River Road.

Distance: 4.2 miles round trip
Portages: Two, both at Miller Street
Parking: Access 16

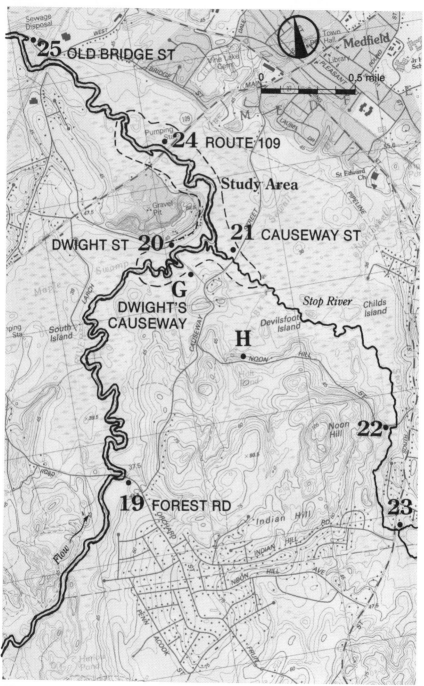

USGS 7.5' × 15': Medfield

Charles River: Towns of Medfield, Millis

Stop River Confluence

Access Points

Canoe

19 FOREST ROAD, Millis (mile 24.4)
USGS Medfield quadrangle
Six cars can be parked in a pulloff to the right of the bridge. One canoe launch is on the upstream right side of the bridge. A good alternative launch site is 100 yards to the east, on the downstream side. Four cars can be parked along the road in this area.

20 DWIGHT STREET, Millis (mile 26.7)
USGS Medfield quadrangle
A gravel parking lot holds ten cars. The launch is below the old bridge abutments.

21 CAUSEWAY STREET, Medfield (mile 27.1)
USGS Medfield quadrangle
Causeway Street crosses Stop River just above its confluence with the Charles. Three cars can be parked along the street. In low water Stop River becomes too shallow for canoes.

22, See "Stop River," page 63.
23

24 ROUTE 109, Medfield (mile 27.9)
USGS Medfield quadrangle
Four cars can be parked in a pulloff on the downstream right side. There is additional parking in pulloffs to the east, but it is more practical to use Access 20 or 25, both of which are nearby.

25 OLD BRIDGE STREET, Medfield (mile 29.0)
USGS Medfield quadrangle
A dozen or more cars can be parked on Old Bridge

Street, which bears north from Bridge Street. The launch is downstream from the bridge on the right bank near Medfield's wastewater treatment plant. Because this location has easy launching, ample off-road parking, and public ownership, it is an excellent access point for canoeists.

Foot

G DWIGHT'S CAUSEWAY and Shattuck Reservation, Medfield
USGS Medfield quadrangle
One-tenth of a mile west of Causeway Street's crossing of Stop River is a narrow road leading into the meadow. At one time this causeway led to Dwight's Bridge. It is an excellent way to walk into the river meadow. Five cars can be parked along the approach to the causeway.

Another tenth of a mile west, a trail leads toward the river. This is the Shattuck Reservation, which includes more than a mile of river frontage.

H See "Stop River," page 63.

Comments
Beginning with this section, the Charles is navigable by canoe at all water levels, though there may be a few scratchy places after prolonged dry weather. Several factors make this part of the river well suited to recreational canoeing. If there should be a spill, the water is clean enough for swimming. The access sites are excellent, much of the land along the banks is conserved, and between the dams in Medway and Natick are twenty portage-free miles.

The river heads north for eight miles through a broad, flat-bottomed valley. This is Area G, the largest area of the Natural Valley Storage Project. Some of the valley floor is red maple swamp. The remainder is wet meadow, spreading to both sides of the Charles and its tributary, Stop River. These meadows attracted Medfield's first settlers because their natural hay was valuable fodder for livestock.

Downstream from Forest Road the river coils into tight meanders. Though the trend is to the north the canoe heads to every point of the compass while following the winding channel. Fin, Fur, and Feathers Sportsman's Club is to the river's left at South Island. Skeet houses are visible from the river. From these, clay pigeons are launched for shotgun practice.

At mile 26.7 the river hurries between the abutments that supported Dwight's Bridge. Access 20 is just below. Dwight's Bridge and Causeway were built before 1700 so that Timothy Dwight could get his hay from the wet meadow. In high water this spot can be difficult for beginners to negotiate, and in low water stones are liable to scratch canoes. Once past Dwight's Bridge, there is flat water all the way to the South Natick Dam. In spring when the water is high and the vegetation low canoeists can see across one-third of a mile of meadow from Dwight's Bridge to Access 21 at Causeway Street.

The mouth of Stop River is reached at mile 27.1. Stop River drains southern Medfield and part of Walpole. About a mile below Stop River, Route 109 intersects the Charles. (It does so twice more in Dedham.) This busy highway crosses the meadows on a causeway. It was constructed as the Boston and Hartford Turnpike, which opened in 1806, when the first bridge was built here. Norfolk County built a concrete bridge in 1909. It was known as "The Willows" because large black willows shaded the road. At that time there was a boathouse here, and the area's first ice cream stand. Canoes were made to order on the premises.

At Access 24 canoes are launched downstream of the bridge, on the right bank. The small parking area limits the value of this launch site. Across the river is a landing at the Charles Restaurant. On weekends this landing is used by Upriver Outfitters, which rents canoes. The proprietor is Larry McCarthy, a knowledgeable advocate of the Charles, who is happy to suggest routes to canoeists. For those wishing to do a one-way trip, car-top carriers are included with the rental, which makes it possible to start here and paddle downstream to South Natick, thus enjoying a particularly pristine and gentle ten-mile section of the Charles. This trip is highly recommended!

Canoeists may land at the Charles Restaurant to refuel, either at the namesake establishment or at the breakfast restaurant next door.

The marsh below Route 109 is particularly attractive to birdlife. Shorebirds are drawn to the mudflats that form when the shallow meadow ponds dry up.

To the north the meadow narrows. Because it is easier to build bridges where the approach is from dry land, Medfield's settlers first bridged the Charles where there was high ground near both banks, at the West Street bridge (mile 29.0). Medfield originally included land to the west of the river which later became the towns of Medway and Millis. Since townspeople lived on both sides, a bridge was needed to unite the town and to allow the Puritans west of the Charles to reach their weekly meeting. By 1653, soon after settlement, the river was spanned. Indians burned this bridge in 1676 during King Philip's War (see page 189). It was rebuilt in 1686 and again in 1784. It was first called "Great Bridge" and later "Brastow's Bridge" and "Poor Farm Bridge," because Medfield's poor farm was located on the present site of the wastewater treatment plant.

The Poor Farm Bridge was near the site of Medfield's original bridge.

Suggested Outings

Canoe

— A downstream trip through this section can be made at a leisurely pace, or can be extended farther downriver for a longer outing.

Distance: 4.6 miles (Forest Road to Old Bridge Street)
Portages: None
Parking:
  Upstream: Access 19
  Downstream: Access 25

— Explore the Stop River Confluence Study Area.
Distance: Variable

Portages: None
Parking: Access 20 or 21, or, if renting a canoe, at the trailer
near the Charles Restaurant on Route 109

Walks
— Visit the river meadows on foot by way of Dwight's
Causeway.
Parking: Access G

Stop River Confluence Study Area

An area rich in forms of life is centered at the mouth of
Stop River. If it flies or swims or thrusts green stems into
Charles River sunlight, look for it here. Life breaks out
late in April, when canoeists may see bumblebees visiting
the white flowers of shadbush, *Amelanchier canadensis.*
The robust bumblebees seen in early spring are queens,
in the sense that they can lay fertile eggs, but these
queens have as yet no court. They were raised the previous autumn by successful bumblebee colonies. The new
queens mated in the sky on Indian summer afternoons,
and stored enough sperm within their bodies to fertilize
all of the eggs they will lay this year. As the weather
cooled, all of the other bees in their colonies perished —
the old queen, the few males, the many workers. Only the
next year's queens live through the winter, to emerge in
early spring.

*Shadbush blooms in early spring, attracting nectar-seeking
bumblebees. Spotted sandpipers, solitary sandpipers, and greater
yellowlegs, are among the shorebirds that hunt invertebrates in the
shallows near the mouth of Stop River.*

57

*Tree swallows, (lower left)
and barn swallows are the
swallow species most
frequently seen along
the Charles.*

Bumblebees can fly in weather too cold for other insects because they can regulate the temperature of their thoraxes. They warm their flight muscles by shivering, and keep them warm by minimizing heat loss. The pile on their bodies insulates them. The control of internal temperature is provided by a heat exchanger that can be turned on and off according to need. In cold temperatures blood flowing from a bee's thorax to her abdomen passes through vessels adjacent to incoming blood, allowing for much of the heat to be transferred. In warm weather the two streams are kept apart so that all of the heat goes into the abdomen and then into the atmosphere through radiation and conduction.

Most of the shrubs along the river's edge produce clusters of white flowers. They bloom in sequence beginning in early spring with shadbush. Shadbush flowers draw bumblebees to the river, where they join a beautiful early-spring butterfly called the mourning cloak in seeking nectar. Because few insects are aloft in April, bumblebees and mourning cloaks draw more notice now than later.

Late April brings the return of the swallows, which make themselves quite conspicuous. They are big enough to be seen at a distance, chatter volubly, sport irridescent plumage, and slice through air with such authority that there seems to be no gap between their intentions and their actions. They eat, drink, bathe, and court on the wing. Their food consists almost entirely of insects, bumblebees and dragonflies included. The open marsh surrounding the mouth of the Stop River is well supplied with swallows. They rest on perches over the water, in mixed flocks consisting primarily of tree and barn swallows, though careful observers will spot bank swallows and the occasional purple martin and rough-winged swallow.

None of the swallows is homely; each species has adherents who think it the best looking. A strong case can be made for the barn swallow. The male has a long forked "swallowtail," which is black with white spots like small panes of milk glass set into a leaded window. His front has contrasting earth tones — a rusty throat, buff below — and his back is irridescent blue-black.

A mid-May morning spent in this study area yielded the song of a wood thrush and sightings of a barn swallow, tree swallow, eastern phoebe, northern mockingbird, yellow warbler, common grackle, red-winged blackbird, great blue heron, red-tailed hawk, gray catbird, northern (Baltimore) oriole, rose-breasted grosbeak, eastern kingbird, mourning dove, American crow, song sparrow, northern cardinal, black-capped chickadee, chimney swift, greater yellowlegs, and several species of sandpipers.

Sandpipers are one of the bird groups that challenge the powers of observation of those who take pleasure in naming the species of a bird rather than placing it in the sandpiper clan and leaving it at that. Four species of sandpipers — solitary, spotted, least, and pectoral — are commonly spotted at the margins of the Charles and its tributaries. Greater and lesser yellowlegs are also seen occasionally, particularly when mud flats have been revealed by a low water level.

Orioles often build their hanging nests above water, and they have done so over the Charles near Dwight's Causeway. By lying on the bottom of the boat, a canoeist can observe and photograph the comings and goings of the birds, their colors vivid in any light but spectacular in May sunbeams, with a deep blue sky for background.

Streamside shrubs include highbush blueberry. When children ask whether these wild blueberries are edible they seem cautious to a fault, but of course the fault is not their own. It indicates that we separate our children from their natural environment, and teach them to fear it. Other shrubs are dogwood, honeysuckle, greenbrier, wild rose, elder, and arrowwood, so named because tradition holds that its straight stems made good arrows. Arrowwood, *Viburnum recognitum,* is an easy shrub to identify, and rewarding because it is often seen. Flat-topped clusters of white flowers open in June. The flower clusters resemble those of elder, but arrowwood blossoms smell like rubber tires, whereas those of elder have a sweet fragrance. The coarse-toothed leaves of arrowwood are simple, in the botanical sense of generating a single leaf from each bud, but elder has compound leaves with three to eleven leaflets each. The margins of elder leaflets are more finely toothed than are the leaves of arrowwood.

Aquatic plants are more readily observed and identified later in the season. By early July they are visible and well developed, and some nesting birds are still feeding their young. Adult eastern kingbirds may be seen struggling to keep up with the demands of ravenous juveniles within a nest in a streamside buttonbush. Buttonbush is at this time beginning to open its spherical clusters of white flowers.

Eastern kingbirds often nest in shrubs at the river's edge.

Giant burreed can be found along the banks. This stout species is in the burreed genus, *Sparganium*. Its three-foot leaves resemble the blades of the streamside grasses, but its flowers are distinctive bur-like balls on crooked stalks. The large burs are female flowers; the small shrivelled ones are male. The seeds and tubers are edible. Although it would impose on wildlife if humans decided to make serious harvests of riverside food stuffs, occasional sampling of the menu offered by the Charles does no harm and is a way of connecting with the natural community and with the hunter-gatherer peoples who lived along the river for thousands of years.

In July the pink buds of smartweed emerge from shallow water. For the rest of the growing season representatives of this genus, *Polygonum*, will be in bloom in one habitat or another. Some *Polygonum* species are called smartweeds; others are called knotweeds. Swamp smartweed grows in and along streams; other species appear in dry locations.

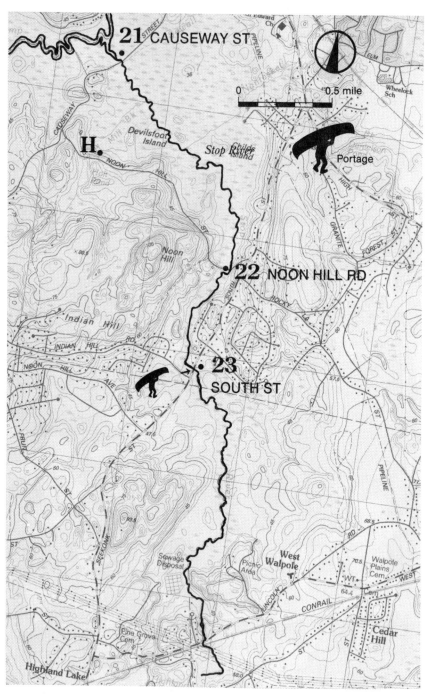

USGS 7.5' × 15': Medfield

Stop River/Charles River: Towns of Medfield, Norfolk, Walpole

Tributary

Stop River

Access Points

Canoe

21 CAUSEWAY STREET, Medfield (mile 27.1)
USGS Medfield quadrangle
Causeway Street crosses Stop River just above its confluence with the Charles. Three cars can be parked along the street. In low water Stop River becomes too shallow for canoes.

22 NOON HILL ROAD, Medfield
USGS Medfield quadrangle
Noon Hill Road crosses Stop River 1.7 miles above its mouth. Six cars can be parked along the road.

23 South Street, Medfield
USGS Medfield quadrangle
Five cars can be parked at South Street, 2.4 miles up Stop River. The launch is upstream of the bridge on the right.

Foot

H NOON HILL RESERVATION, Medfield
USGS Medfield quadrangle
This property of The Trustees of Reservations has a parking lot for four cars on Noon Hill Street.

Comments
Early in Medfield's history, its farmers constructed causeways into their river meadows. This effort must have required enormous labor, but hay was a vital energy source for their draft animals, and the causeways were needed to bring wagons to the hay. Dwight's Causeway is mentioned in Medfield records for 1660; Causeway Street probably preceded it. Today the Causeway Street bridge has wooden beams and railings. Five cars can be parked by the pussy willow in the adjacent pulloff. In low water, shoals near the bridge interfere with navigation. When water is moderate or high the mouth of Stop River can be entered from the Charles.

One-fifth of a mile upstream, Sawmill Brook enters on Stop River's left. Access H is up this brook near the mill pond. Noon Hill rises prominently to the south. Because the hill is so distinct and is on the southern side of town, Medfield's early residents could tell it was dinner time when the sun was over Noon Hill.

In the wooded swamp to the right of the stream are two steep-sided islands. The second of these is nearer the channel. Named after its cloven-stone topography, Devilsfoot Island is worth a landing. It is about 125 yards long and 50 yards wide. The easiest landing is at the upstream end of the island. In late April, the following birds were seen during a short visit: palm warbler, ruby-crowned kinglet, hairy woodpecker, brown creeper, northern mockingbird, and tree swallow. From the canoe, several other species were added to the list for this outing: common grackle, American crow, red-winged blackbird, red-tailed hawk, white-throated sparrow, eastern phoebe, and Canada goose. The latter were distributed in pairs at intervals along the stream. Toads were heard trilling from the direction of Noon Hill. The trees on Devilsfoot Island are white pines, beeches, and oaks. The site of a cabin that burned in 1982 is marked by its foundation and chimney.

Just above Devilsfoot Island, Nantasket Brook enters from Stop River's right. Childs Island is on the same side, opposite a tongue of high ground that protrudes from Noon Hill.

Noon Hill Street is 1.7 miles above the Charles. Because John Frairy reached his meadow on the Stop River from a bridge he built here in 1653, it was known as Frairy's Bridge. It was rebuilt in 1829. The pretty stone bridge was washed out in 1990 and was replaced with concrete culverts.

A big winterberry bush is above the bridge, near a black willow in repose across the stream. There are houses near the stream on its right bank until the South Street bridge is reached 2.4 miles above the Charles. This bridge is of unusual construction. A pier of stacked stones supports the ends of long slabs of granite that reach out from the abutments on either side. The bridge is too low to paddle under, and the short portage is complicated by heavy traffic on South Street. The portage is on the left side of the stream.

Above South Street, Stop River is the boundary between Norfolk and Walpole. In the summer, canoeists attempting to paddle the narrow channel upstream of South Street may find their passage barred by thick mats of floating duckweed. With effort, canoes can be forced through these barriers, but their odor is offensive. Such blooms of duckweed are caused by an excess of nutrients in the water. Marsh wrens nest in the extensive stands of cattail on this section of Stop River. A skeet house on the grounds of the Walpole Sportsman's Association is visible across the marsh to the south.

The head of navigation is reached four miles above the Charles, just above a wastewater treatment plant, near the crossing of the power lines.

Suggested Outings

Canoe
— Paddle upstream and back from Causeway Street. Moderate or high water is required.
Distance: 8.2 miles round trip
Portages: Two, both at South Street
Parking: Access 21

Walks
— Hike to the summit of Noon Hill on the trail at Noon Hill Reservation. Side trips within the reservation can extend this hike.
Distance, round trip: 1.4 miles up a moderate grade
Parking: Access H

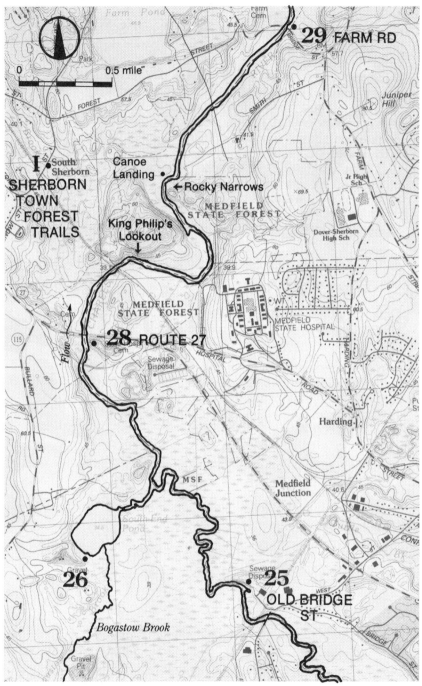

USGS 7.5' × 15': Medfield

Charles River: Towns of Dover, Medfield, Millis, Sherborn

Rocky Narrows

Access Points

Canoe

25 OLD BRIDGE STREET, Medfield (mile 29.0)
USGS Medfield quadrangle
A dozen or more cars can be parked on Old Bridge
Street, which bears north from Bridge Street. The launch
is downstream from the bridge on the right bank near
Medfield's wastewater treatment plant. Because this
location has easy launching, ample off-road parking, and
public ownership, it is an excellent access point.

26, 27 See Bogastow Brook, page 73.

28 ROUTE 27, Medfield (mile 31.8)
USGS Medfield quadrangle
Canoes can be launched from the river's right bank,
upstream of the bridge. Six or more cars can be parked
along the road.

29 FARM ROAD, Sherborn (Bridge Street, Dover) (mile
34.3)
USGS Medfield quadrangle
A boat launch and off-road parking area are downstream
of the bridge on the right side of the river. A dozen cars
can be parked here.

Foot

I SHERBORN TOWN FOREST TRAILS
USGS Medfield quadrangle
An extensive network of trails can be reached from the
trailhead on Forest Street. Hikers can reach King Philip's
Lookout and The Trustees of Reservations canoe landing
at Rocky Narrows. To purchase a trail map, write the
Sherborn Forest and Trail Association, PO Box 477, Sherborn, Massachusetts, 01770. There is no parking at the
trailhead. One answer to this problem is to arrive by
bicycle. Another is to park elsewhere in the
neighborhood and walk to the trailhead.

Comments

Below Bridge Street the Charles passes through the lower half of the Medfield meadows, also known as Area G of the Natural Valley Storage Project. Area G totals 2,656 acres. Bluejoint grass predominates in the open wet meadow. The Massachusetts Division of Fisheries and Wildlife manages this land, and puts about 3,300 trout into the Charles between Medway and South Natick, either brook trout or brown trout. Snowshoe rabbits are released in the Great Black Swamp, and pheasant are stocked in the river marshes near Route 27.

Trout are also stocked in Bogastow Brook, which joins the Charles from the left at mile 30.5. South End Pond, a quarter of a mile up the brook, was the site of a fortified house in which early Millis and Sherborn settlers successfully resisted attack during King Philip's War (see page 192). Bogastow Brook is the Charles River's largest tributary. It drains much of Millis, Holliston, and Sherborn, and has a flow equal to that of the Charles above Medway. For additional information about Bogastow Brook, see page 73.

The valley narrows and the great meadow is left behind. The abutments of a bygone bridge pinch the channel at mile 31.6. This was Death's Bridge. Henry Death bought a farm on the Sherborn side in 1777, and the bridge took his family name, but a bridge here had linked Sherborn and Medfield before King Philip's War. It was destroyed by the Indians to discourage pursuit as they retreated to the west from their raid on Medfield in February of 1676. The text of the note they left at the bridge is on page 190.

Route 27's steel and concrete bridge is the sort that gives the twentieth century a bad name: all practicality with nothing to spare for aesthetics. Pigeons like it; the I-beams are wide enough for their nests. Below Route 27 is a railroad bridge in active use by Conrail.

The Charles becomes less curly as its valley narrows. There is a series of relatively straight reaches. The first is from Route 27 to "King Philip's Lookout," a wall of bedrock rising one hundred feet above the river. The rock is rhyolite, a fine-grained igneous rock about 650 million years old. The steepness of the hills in the Rocky Narrows area tells part of their story. Unlike the gently rounded clay-and-gravel hills created by glaciers, the hills at the Narrows are made of tough old rock.

The bluff below King Philip's Lookout whisks the
Charles River to the right, and it flows along a stone face as
straight as if it were laid out by an engineer. The river
skirts to the right of the hill, and then passes a marsh on
the left. A backwater indents this marsh. In the woods
above the backwater is a gigantic boulder that offers an
overhang large enough to shelter a family from the
elements. Here was a natural way station for those whose
canoe journeys did not begin and end at automobiles. Hun-
ters from a prehistoric village at Populatic Pond might have
floated down to this point in the space of a day, using their
dugout canoes as blinds. At the overhang the hunter could
roast a duck, protected from snow or rain, resting for the
arduous paddle back to Populatic Pond.

Rocky Narrows (mile 33.2) is a short stretch in which
the river has steep wooded banks on both sides, with large
exposures of ledge, particularly on the right bank. The left
bank is a conical hill, an island separated by a c-shaped
swath of marsh from the vertical rock hillside beyond.
Apparently this marsh was the river channel until natural
forces cut off the meander at its neck and Rocky Narrows
was formed.

Canoes can be landed on the right bank upstream of the
rocky promontory to picnic or to explore the hemlock-clad
slopes of Medfield State Forest, near Medfield State Hospital. It is also possible to land on the island on the left, which
has marsh on three sides and the river on the fourth.

A landing belonging to The Trustees of Reservations is
on the left bank below the Narrows. This organization was
established in 1891 by landscape architect Charles Eliot.
The Trustees of Reservations' purpose is to preserve
Massachusetts properties of scenic, historic, and ecological
value. Members are supplied a guide to properties. For
information call (508) 921-1944 or write The Trustees of
Reservations, 572 Essex Street, Beverly, Massachusetts,
01915. Groups are occasionally permitted to camp at the
canoe landing at Rocky Narrows. To apply for permission,
send a letter of request to The Trustees of Reservations,
Box 352, Medfield, Massachusetts, 02052.

The Rocky Narrows Reservation abuts the Sherborn
Town Forest, which includes King Philip's Lookout, and
good foot trails lead from one to the other.

Opposite the canoe landing is a town boundary. Medfield, which has been on the river's right bank, gives way to

Dover. The left bank continues as Sherborn. These three towns have notably low population densities. Sherborn's is 216 people per square mile; Dover's is 302 per square mile, and Medfield, urban by comparison, has 716 per square mile. Cambridge and Boston each has more than 12,000 residents per square mile. As it passes between Dover and Sherborn, the Charles enters a district of estates. The Trustees of Reservations owns conservation restrictions on some estates, and the Massachusetts Audubon Society holds conservation easements for parts of others. The owners of these estates and the conservation organizations have found ways to cooperate in preserving this portion of the river corridor, to the benefit of wildlife and canoeists who enjoy the tranquil riverbanks.

The reach between Rocky Narrows and Farm Road is frequented by red-tailed hawks.

A solitary upstream canoe trip began at Farm Road on an early spring morning. Approaching the Narrows, this paddler heard human voices chanting in the distance. As minutes passed, the sound grew nearer; the canoe and the people seemed to be travelling on converging lines. In March, foliage does not obstruct the view; spots of color became visible between the trees. A single file of adults in gray sweat-suits marched into sight wearing red-orange stocking caps. At the head of the line, a bright blue flag snapped in the breeze. Chanting continued as a zig zag course brought the marchers to the brow of rock at Rocky Narrows. The observer supposed that a human sacrifice might ensue, but the apparition turned out to be the morning exercise of corrections officers being trained on the grounds of Medfield State Hospital.

Suggested Outings

Canoe
— Canoe downstream from Old Bridge Street to Farm Road, or continue to South Natick. This part of the Charles is deservedly popular with canoeists. Conservation land and estates along the banks make it the most rural section, and the water is ample and flat.
Distance: 5.3 miles (Old Bridge Street to Farm Road)
Portages: None
Parking:
  Upstream: Access 25
  Downstream: Access 29 or 31

— Paddle to Rocky Narrows from Sherborn's Farm Road. This is an excellent family outing with picnicking and hiking opportunities at the Narrows. Canoes can land on the river's left bank at The Trustees of Reservations site or landings can be improvised near the steep-sided Narrows, and lunch can be enjoyed on the hemlock-shaded hills. There are good trails within reach of The Trustees of Reservations landing.
Distance: 2.2 miles round trip
Portages: None
Parking: Access 29

— South End Pond, a natural pond in Millis, is the destination of another good family canoe trip. Its landing is listed on page 73 as an access point for Bogastow Brook, but it is more exciting to approach the pond in a canoe than in a car.
Distance: 3.2 miles round trip
Portages: None
Parking: Access 28

Walks
— Hike to King Philip's Lookout. The sweeping view from the crest includes the Charles and the fields and woods of Medfield State Forest. Noon Hill is visible in the distance to the south. The round trip walking distance from The Trustees of Reservations canoe landing at Rocky Narrows to the crest of the bluff is 1.8 miles. The lookout can be reached on foot from Access I.

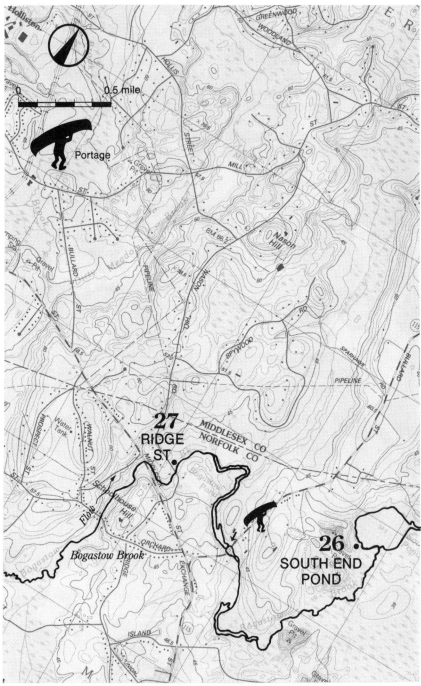

USGS 7.5′× 15′: Framingham, Medfield

Bogastow Brook/Charles River: Town of Millis

Tributary

Bogastow Brook

Access Points

Canoe

26 SOUTH END POND, Millis
USGS Medfield quadrangle
Seven cars can be parked at the landing on the west edge
of the pond, which is reached by a gravel road from
Orchard Street.

27 RIDGE STREET, Millis
USGS Medfield quadrangle
The launch is downstream of the bridge, on the left. Two
cars will fit along the road.

Comments

South End pond is in northern Millis, but it was originally
thought to be within the south end of Sherborn. It is sometimes called Bogastow Pond. The battles at South End Pond
are described on page 192.

A pleasing variety of plants border Bogastow Brook.
Botanically minded canoeists should explore here. To
ascend Bogastow Brook, canoeists enter the west side of the
pond at Access 26 and paddle into the inlet on the south
side. Silt from the brook has built a marshy delta where it
flows into the pond. Common plants near the brook's mouth
include buttonbush, purple loosestrife, wild rose, cardinal
flower, kinnikinnick, forget-me-not, and wild grape. In July,
deerflies can be pesky.

Patches of woods are encountered on the way upstream.
A shrub called buckthorn grows at a pool shaded by red
maple and American elm. Two ferns are seen: royal fern
where there is some shade, and sensitive fern in full sun.
Poison ivy prefers shade, but vines of bitter nightshade
climb shrubs in the brightest light.

There is a cornfield on the brook's left.

Clumps of yellow iris appear at intervals along Bogastow. Damselflies patrol the water's surface, and great blue herons hunt its shallows; in summertime, deer hide in cool, shady places along the stream. One and one-quarter miles above the pond, a footbridge spans the stream at the homestead of Joseph Daniel, the second white settler of Millis. Near a sharp bend in the brook, on a high bank to the stream's right, stands the house Joseph Daniel built in 1676 to replace the one burned by the Indians. The barn, said to have been spared by the Indians out of consideration for the family, is thought to pre-date 1660 and is perhaps the oldest building in Millis. It has been converted to housing, and contains several unique apartments.

Orchard Street (Route 115) is another half mile upstream, past Cassidy's farm. The channel is split below the road. Canoeists continuing upstream should take the channel to the brook's left, and carry up to Orchard Street. Be careful — this road is heavily travelled. Cross Orchard Street and cross the brook's left fork. A path leads to the old mill dam on the right fork.

In 1686 Joseph Daniel was given permission to build a mill dam at this site. The mill at Orchard Street served a variety of purposes for many years. In 1874 there were saw and grist mills here, owned by Michael Henry Collins, a successful inventor. He built the house on the right bank, #9 on the Millis Historic Trail, overlooking the dam and mills. The millpond came to be called Collins' Pond. The pond has grown up with vegetation, including great bulrush, narrow- and broad-leaved cattails, smartweed, alder, buckthorn, grape, meadowsweet, yellow iris, highbush blueberry, pickerelweed, and red maple.

Ridge Street is 1.2 miles above Orchard Street. In 1693 Joseph Daniel Junior came to live here. He built a sawmill and later a grist mill. These operated for over 140 years but were abandoned in the 1850s to increase the flow at the Orchard Street Dam. The bridge at Ridge Street was called the Grist Mill Bridge. Above Ridge Street, Bogastow Brook winds through the Great Black Swamp, where numerous fallen trees make canoeing impractical. Bogastow Brook can be visited on foot where it passes under the railroad arches on Woodland Street in Holliston.

Suggested Outings

Canoe

— Paddle upstream from South End Pond to Orchard Street. High or medium water is preferable.
Distance: 3.5 miles
Portages: None
Parking: Access 26

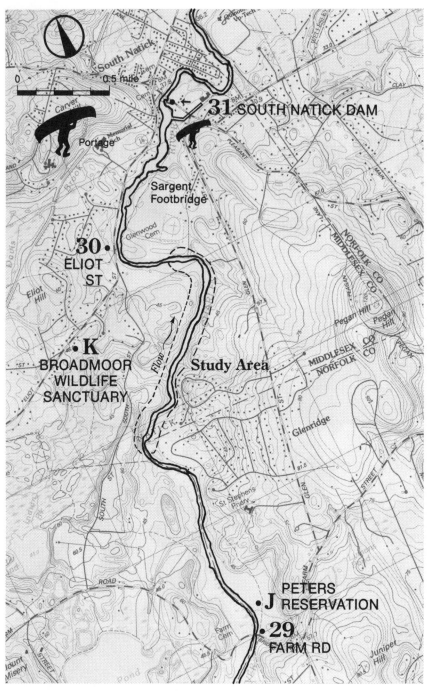

31 SOUTH NATICK DAM

Sargent Footbridge

30 ELIOT ST

K BROADMOOR WILDLIFE SANCTUARY

Study Area

J PETERS RESERVATION

29 FARM RD

Portage

USGS 7.5' × 15': Framingham, Medfield

Charles River: Dover, Natick, Sherborn

Broadmoor

Access Points

Canoe

29 FARM ROAD, Sherborn (Bridge Street, Dover)
(mile 34.3)
USGS Medfield quadrangle
There is a boat launch downstream of the bridge on the
right side of the river. The parking area will accomodate
a dozen cars.

30 ELIOT STREET, (Route 16) Natick (mile 37.0)
USGS Framingham quadrangle
Canoes can be launched at a dirt pulloff between the
road and the river's left bank. The pulloff, which has
room for five cars, is too muddy to use in wet conditions.
There is no intersection here. The pulloff is near the
crossing of the power lines and across the river from an
exposure of ledge.

31 SOUTH NATICK DAM (mile 37.8)
USGS Framingham quadrangle
A small park on the right bank offers good canoe
launches both above and below the South Natick Dam.
Ten cars can be parked along busy Pleasant Street, which
crosses the river below the dam. Off-road parking is
available at the end of Merrill Road, near the athletic
fields on the other side of Pleasant Street.

Foot

J PETERS RESERVATION, Dover
USGS Medfield quadrangle
Good trails are maintained by The Trustees of Reser-
vations. Parking is at Access 29.

K BROADMOOR WILDLIFE SANCTUARY, Eliot Street,
Natick
USGS Framingham quadrangle

Dozens of cars can be parked in the gravel lot at the headquarters of this Massachusetts Audubon Society sanctuary. Visitors pay a small admission fee at the office and are lent a trail map. The refuge is open dawn to dusk, Tuesday through Sunday. There are about nine miles of trails.

Comments

The Trustees of Reservations' 91-acre Peters Reservation is on the right bank for nearly half a mile below Farm Road. A sign marks the canoe landing. The reservation has good foot trails.

An old bridge abutment is on the right bank at mile 34.9. Doverites called this Wight's Bridge, after the family that farmed the land here. The bridge was built around 1820 by Hezekiah and Leonard Morse of Sherborn. The silo and buildings on the left are part of Charlescoate Farm, a large private estate.

At mile 35.4 the river bends to the right in front of a steep bank. Here the Charles leaves Sherborn and Dover, and enters Natick. Broadmoor Wildlife Sanctuary begins on the left bank, and continues for a mile on that side. Past the contemporary houses on the right, Broadmoor owns both banks for half a mile. Broadmoor is owned by the Massachusetts Audubon Society, which was the first Audubon Society in the country. The purpose of Massachusetts Audubon is to preserve an environment that supports both human beings and wildlife through conservation, education, research, and advocacy. For membership information call (508) 655-2296 or write Massachusetts Audubon at Broadmoor Wildlife Sanctuary, 280 Eliot Street, South Natick, Massachusetts, 01760. Broadmoor's riverbanks are the study area below.

At mile 36.5 the Charles turns ninety degrees to the left, runs straight for half a mile, then turns squarely back to the right. This stretch is rocky in low water. Access 30 is on the left near the power lines. Route 16 (Eliot Street) runs parallel to the left bank.

Harvard professor Daniel Sargent purchased property on both sides of the Charles in 1921. He placed a statue on the right bank in 1929. It portrays the Virgin Mary overcoming evil, symbolized by the snake beneath her feet. The statue was carved in Indiana limestone by John H. Benson. The words "Apparverunt in terra nostra flores" ("The flowers shall appear on our earth") are inscribed in the pedestal. Sargent planted rhododendrons along the river's right bank, upstream of the footbridge at mile 37.3. These bloom at different times in different colors, so visitors find them in flower throughout the late spring and early summer. Sargent built a footbridge on the foundations of the dam that Thomas Sawin was compelled to remove in 1723 (see page 190).

The intake canal for the South Natick mill is one-fifth of a mile above the dam. The dam itself is potentially hazardous to careless boaters. Canoes can be landed in the park, on the right bank. For through-paddlers, the portage is a short one; canoes are carried across the little park and returned to the river below the dam but above the bridge. This bridge of four stone arches was built in 1857 at a cost of $3442.42.

Oldtown Park is to the left of the dam. The name "Oldtown" refers to Harriet Beecher Stowe's novel, *Oldtown Folks,* written in 1869, which is set in South Natick in the 1790s. During visits to her inlaws, who lived in a house in the village, Stowe became acquainted with many of the characters she portrayed in the novel.

The park is on the site of a fulling mill operated by Hezekiah Broad around 1733. The Bigelow family had paper, saw, and grist mills here around 1800. In 1838 the dam was raised and a canal built to carry water to a paper mill. In the 1890s electricity was generated at this site, but the water supply was insufficient, so the privilege was sold to a company that made bedding. Water wheels turned here as late as 1918. The present dam was completed September 1, 1934.

The historical significance of South Natick is described beginning on page 183.

Suggested Outings

Canoe

— Canoe downstream through this section. This can be done as a quick paddle or it can be floated slowly and quietly in order to observe birds and other wildlife. Often this section is the final leg of trips that begin in Medway, Millis, or Medfield.
Distance: 3.5 miles
Portages: None
Parking:
    Upstream: Access 29
    Downstream: Access 31

— From Eliot Street, paddle through Broadmoor Wildlife Sanctuary.
Distance: Variable, up to five miles round trip
Portages: None
Parking: Access 30

Walks

— The Charles River Trail at Broadmoor Wildlife Sanctuary is one of the best places to visit the river on foot.
Parking: Access K

— The Peters Reservation, once a private estate, has extensive trails maintained by The Trustees of Reservations.
Parking: Access 29

Great horned owls are occasionally seen on pine boughs over the river at Broadmoor Wildlife Sanctuary.

Broadmoor Wildlife Sanctuary Study Area

Opposite the Natick-Medfield boundary the Charles is deflected to the right by a steep ridge. South Street runs along the top of the ridge, linking Sherborn's Farm Road with Eliot Street (Route 16) in Natick, and bisecting the 732-acre Broadmoor Wildlife Sanctuary. The Sanctuary property has a 300 year history. The Indian citizens of Natick, tired of carrying their grain a long distance to be milled, decided to invite a friendly and mechanically inclined white resident of Sherborn, Thomas Sawin, to move to Natick and construct a mill. This Sawin did around 1692, taking up his grant of land and water rights and becoming the town's first non-Indian resident. The brook he used for power flows from Little Farm Pond to the Charles. It became known as Sawin Brook, but is now called Indian Brook.

Around 1720 Thomas Sawin and his son John built a larger dam that made a greater pond, which they used to power grist mills and sawmills. These mills stayed in the family until 1858 when they were purchased by John Andrew Morse, who continued operation through the turn of the century. Mrs. Marion Pfeiffer recalled the Morse era:

> Sixty years ago [in 1899] the mills were a busy place. In winter we saw logs being hauled to the sawmill and all year around the farmers took their corn to be ground. It wasn't always easy for my father to leave his farm work in fall or spring so my brothers, my sister and I as we grew older took our turn at driving the horse and wagon with five or six bushels of field corn on the cob to be ground with oats, which we usually bought from Mr. Morse, into feed for the farm animals.
>
> I remember Mr. Morse very well. He was quite deaf and very lame from rheumatism; he used one cane even when I was a child and later he used two. At the mill he always wore blue overalls and jumper and an old straw hat of the narrow brim variety. His beard was very white as was his rim of white hair. The top of his head was completely bald. His eyes were a clear bright blue and piercing, his cheeks quite pink and he always was scrupulously clean.
>
> (from "The Morse Mills at South Natick" by Marion Pfeiffer, 1959.)

Preston Morse, son of John Andrew and Deborah Bullard Morse, established a machine shop beneath the mill. Despite a hand mutilated by an accident in the sawmill, Preston Morse was an expert machinist and a suc-

81

cessful inventor, abreast of the technology of the day. Decades before they were in common use, telephones were installed for communication between the mill and the house. In 1929 Preston Morse sold the property to Carl Stillman. Broadmoor became what it is today when land from the Stillman family was added to the original acreage at Sherborn's Little Farm Pond, which had been donated by Henry S. Channing in 1962.

Broadmoor Sanctuary is managed primarily for the benefit of wildlife, and secondarily for human visitors. There is no canoe landing at the refuge; visitors enter from Eliot Street where there is plenty of parking. Maps to the nine miles of trails are available in the visitors' center. One trail crosses the old dam. The stone millraces the Sawins built to carry water to and from their mills bear silent testimony to the great labors of our forebearers.

The red-tailed hawk is the bird of prey most likely to be observed in the valley of the Charles.

An excellent walk along the river is offered by the Charles River Trail, which takes advantage of Broadmoor's high, firm riverbank. It is only in such places that white pines grow close to the river, because they require footing in well-drained soil. The tall pines sometimes shelter birds of prey. For several seasons red-tailed hawks have occupied a riverside nest in this area, and great horned owls occasionally pass the hours of daylight in Broadmoor's pines within sight of passing canoeists. With a wingspread of four feet and weighing up to four and a half pounds, the female great horned owl is the mistress of the New England darkness. Great horned owls mate for life. They nest from late February to mid-April, the twenty-eight day incubation shared by males and females. Most of their hooting is done in late winter, at the beginning of the nesting season. The Massachusetts ornithologist Edward Howe Forbush wrote of the great horned owl:

> We can hardly wonder that certain Indian tribes regarded this fowl as the very personification of the Evil One, or that they feared its influence and regarded its visits to their dwellings as portentous of disaster or death.
>
> The courtship of the Horned Owl is a curious performance. The male goes through peculiar contortions, nodding, bowing, flapping its wings and using, meanwhile, the choicest and most persuasive owl language. One motion which seems common to all owls is a rotary movement of the head which is raised to the full length of the neck, then swung to one side and dropped as low at least as the feet, and then swung to the other side and raised again, giving the owl a ludicrous appearance. Whatever may be said about the fierceness and ferocity of owls, no one can accuse them of being unfaithful to their young. Mr. Farley tells me that more than once he has found the nest well lined with a handsome, yellow mass of warm feathers from the mother's breast which seemed analogous to the downy lining of a duck's nest. She sits closely on her eggs during the cold days and long nights of late February and early March. Often the snow covers both her and the nest and then if she is driven away by an intruder the nest will be found covered with snow surrounding the imprint of her body, showing where she has faithfully outstayed the storm. The young remain in the nest and continue to grow for one long month, and during all that time they are well cared for and provided with a quantity of food.
>
> (from *Birds of Massachusetts and Other New England States*, Volume II, by Edward Howe Forbush)

Great horned owls prey on skunks and consequently often smell of them. This owl's menu includes most animals between the sizes of a goose and a mouse. Snakes, crows, grouse, ducks, songbirds, woodchucks, weasels, rabbits, squirrels, rats, opossums, and even fish are killed by great horned owls. In all likelihood the surface of the Charles at Broadmoor is occasionally broken by the talons of one of these powerful predators as it snatches a fish that lingered too near the surface.

Great horned owls rarely build nests; perhaps some year a family of owls will inherit the nest red-tailed hawks have constructed on the right bank of the Charles near Broadmoor. The red-tailed hawk is the bird of prey most likely to be observed in the valley of the Charles and for that matter in most of North America east of the Rocky Mountains. It is rare to travel down the Broadmoor, Rocky Narrows, or Stop River Confluence sections of the Charles without seeing one. They are grayish brown above, and mostly white below. Mature birds boast the red tail which is easily seen when sunlight passes through it. It is the red of the robin's breast, not the red of the cardinal.

The largest red-tailed hawk falls a little short of the largest great horned owl in weight and wing span. The biggest individuals of both species are females weighing approximately four pounds. Red-tails feed largely on field mice. They usually hunt by patient watching from a perch such as a dead limb from which they can view several acres of mouse habitat. The cry of the red-tail conveys a pure defiant wildness; the shrill *kee-aahrr-r-r-r* lifts the eyes to a hawk far above. To conserve energy, red-tails soar as much as possible, rarely flapping their wings. Instead, using their broad wing surfaces, they catch currents of rising air, which they ride to great heights before gliding to another updraft. Migrating hawks cover many miles in this manner. This is solar-powered travel; the sun heats the Earth's surface, warming the lowest layers of air, which flows upward in columns.

Often humans locate hawks and owls not by the sounds of their own calls but by the rancorous gangs of crows and jays that harass them.

The Massachusetts Audubon Society organizes canoe trips down the Charles, and keeps track of bird species seen during these outings. The following birds were seen from canoes in the Broadmoor area between 1987 and 1990: double-crested cormorant, great blue heron, green-backed heron, black-crowned night heron, Canada goose, mallard, bufflehead, northern goshawk, sharp-shinned hawk, red-tailed and broad-winged hawks, osprey, American kestrel, killdeer, spotted sandpiper, great black-backed gull, rock dove, mourning dove, great horned owl, chimney swift, belted kingfisher, northern flicker, pileated woodpecker, hairy woodpecker, downy wood-pecker, eastern kingbird, eastern phoebe, tree swallow, barn swallow, blue jay, American crow, black-capped chickadee, tufted titmouse, white-breasted nuthatch, gray catbird, American robin, cedar waxwing, European starling, black-and-white warbler, northern parula, yellow warbler, yellow-rumped warbler, common yellowthroat, red-winged blackbird, northern oriole, common grackle, American goldfinch, scarlet tanager, rose-breasted gros-beak, and song sparrow.

The pileated wood-pecker has a brilliant red crest and vivid white markings.

At Broadmoor the big forest trees grow right down to the river. Some of these trees are dead, and their slowly decomposing trunks play vital roles in the forest ecosystem. Hollows shelter birds and mammals, and the wood feeds insects that nourish woodpeckers. Woodpeckers do not migrate; they keep us company throughout the year, adding stout-hearted life to the gray winter forest. At Broadmoor, downy woodpeckers and hairy woodpeckers are most often seen. Because it is not common in New England, encountering a pileated woodpecker is a special pleasure. If seen, the pileated woodpecker will not be mistaken for anything else. It is nearly as large as a crow and has a prominent flaming red crest. Vivid white markings on its face, neck, and wings stand out from the slate-black background plumage. Its call is a loud, emphatic *cock cock cock* that resounds through the woods.

Like other woodpeckers, the pileated is adapted to detect and extract the myriads of wood-boring insects within dead or dying wood. It excavates large cavities in trees to raise its young and to keep safe from owls in winter. The hollows created by pileated woodpeckers are large enough to serve, in subsequent years, as nest cavities for wood ducks.

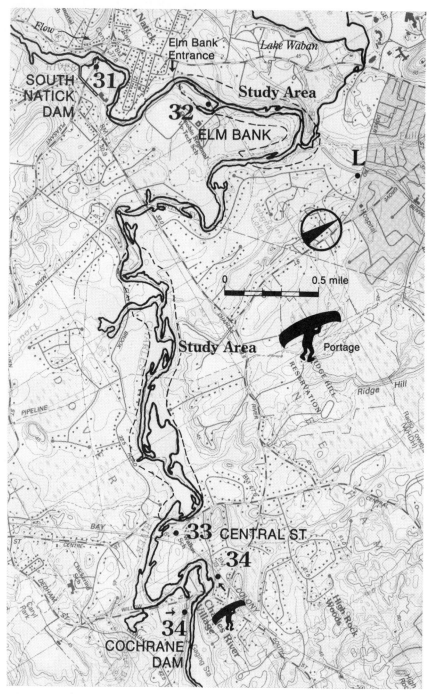

USGS 7.5'× 15': Framingham, Medfield

Charles River: Towns of Dover, Natick, Needham, Wellesley

Bays Region

Access Points

Canoe

31 SOUTH NATICK DAM (mile 37.8)
USGS Framingham quadrangle
A small park on the river's right offers good canoe
launches both above and below the South Natick Dam.
Ten cars can be parked along busy Pleasant Street, which
crosses the river below the dam. Off-road parking is
available at the end of Merrill Road, near the athletic
fields on the other side of Pleasant Street.

32 ELM BANK, Dover (mile 39.0)
USGS Framingham quadrangle
At present, this Metropolitan District Commission park is
open Wednesday through Sunday, from 9 A.M. to dusk.
The park is entered from Washington Street (Route 16)
in Wellesley. Cars cross the Charles on the narrow
Cheney Bridge, turn right onto the one-way road through
the property, and circle back nearly to the entrance
before reaching the canoe launch. The grass parking area
holds ten cars. Elm Bank offers excellent walking trails
along the Charles.

33 CENTRAL STREET, Needham (mile 43.4)
USGS Framingham quadrangle
The launch is at a pulloff on the Needham side of the
river one-fifth of a mile above the bridge. There is room
for three cars.

34 COCHRANE DAM, Dover (mile 44.5)
USGS Framingham quadrangle
Canoeists arriving from upstream should land at
Redwing Bay, at Fisher Street, on the left bank upstream
of the bridge. A major public works project currently
disrupts access to the boat ramp, but it is expected to be
restored when construction is over. The road crossing
the bridge is Willow Street in Dover and South Street in
Needham. The downstream launch is on the opposite
side of the river, on Mill Street (see page 105).

Foot

L   DOVER ROAD, Wellesley
USGS Framingham quadrangle
Pedestrians atop the Sudbury Aqueduct get a nice view
from the Waban Arches and access to trails along the
river. Parking is difficult because there is no pulloff and
the shoulder is quite narrow near the aqueduct, but on-
road parking is possible a few hundred feet southeast of
the aqueduct. *See also:* Access 32.

Comments
The Charles flows briskly over the smooth gravel bed below
Pleasant Street. It passes to the rear of the Eliot Montessori
School then bends to the right, skirting South Natick
homes, where it receives water that passed through the mill
canal. A modern building on the site is occupied by Ealing
Company, which manufactures precision pumps for scien-
tific and medical uses.

The Cheney Bridge is at mile 38.6. It was constructed in
1897 to replace a wooden bridge. It is a single arch of steel,
with decorative ironwork including wrought-iron lamp posts
at the corners. The bridge was reconditioned in 1990. It
provides access to Elm Bank, a state-owned property with
two miles of frontage on the right bank of the Charles. The
Elm Bank canoe launch is on the right, near the mouth of a
canal that supplied water to an ornamental pond and a boat
house. At Elm Bank, the riverbanks are relatively high,
fringed with shrubs, and shaded by mature trees. The
shrubs include alder, sweet pepperbush, elder, and winterberry. The trees are white oak, red maple, white pine, and
river birch. On the left bank, opposite the tip of the Elm
Bank peninsula, swamp azalea, greenbrier, and tupelo add
variety to the plant life.

The Charles is fairly broad here, thirty to forty yards.
The current is strongest in the middle. At the edges the
water is slack, slowed by friction with the bank. When a
heavy mid-summer rain sets the duckweed in motion it is
easy to see the variations in speed.

It is marshy at the mouth of Waban Brook (mile 39.4).
Purple loosestrife grows here, plus swamp loosestrife (also
called water willow). The Waban Arches can be glimpsed to
the left. They were built by the Boston Water Works in 1876
to support the Sudbury Aqueduct, which carried water from
a reservoir in Framingham to Chestnut Hill Reservoir in

Boston. The top of Waban Arches is reached from Access L.
In high water it is possible to canoe up Waban Brook to
Lake Waban (see page 101).

The Charles turns south toward the Bays Region. These
backwaters are abandoned channels formed as the river
wriggled at the bottom of its valley. Charles River Street
crosses at mile 40.9 near the site of an old Indian fish weir.
The Bays Region stretches three and one-half miles, from
Charles River Street to the Cochrane Dam. The river is
flanked with expensive real estate. Several of the houses
seen from the river are very large, truly mansions, set high
on the sides of the valley. Others, like the contemporary at
the hair pin turn just below Charles River Street, are right
beside the river.

Clay Brook Road is on the right at mile 41.5, and the
mouth of Trout Brook is three-tenths of a mile beyond. In
the 1600s, clay for bricks was extracted from a pit in this
area.

The long arm of marsh separating the Charles from the
largest bay supports a lush stand of reed canarygrass.

Access 33 on Central Street is reached before the
bridge, which is a picturesque structure of three arches of
stone and concrete with white wooden rails. The Bay
Colony Railroad bridge is just beyond. Between the two is a
striking structure, the main academic building of the Walker
School.

Noanet Brook enters through a culvert passing beneath
Willow Street at mile 43.9. Noanet Brook drains the hills of
central Dover. On the left is the Charles River Peninsula,
twenty-nine acres owned by The Trustees of Reservations
which was formerly the Walker-Gordon Dairy Farm. The
upstream landing of Access 34 is at Redwing Bay. The
South Street-Willow Street bridge is a few yards above the
dam. The portage is a long one, from Redwing Bay across
the bridge to Mill Street.

Suggested Outings

Canoe

— On a downstream trip through this section, the scenery
varies between woods, marsh, and attractive houses. This
part of the river is quiet because it is far from highways.
Distance: 6.7 miles
Portages: None

Parking:
    Upstream: Access 31 (or behind Ealing Company
    if available)
    Downstream: Access 34

— Explore Elm Bank and the mouth of Waban Brook.
Here is excellent boating for families and novices. The
scenery is forest, accented by the architecture of Elm
Bank and the Waban Arches.
Distance: Variable
Portages: None
Parking: Access 32

Walks
— Elm Bank provides ideal walking along the Charles
River because it has parking, public ownership, a quiet
natural setting, and an extensive system of good trails.
Parking: Access 32, or at other parking areas near
the trails

— Visit Waban Arches, and explore the trails nearby.
Parking: Access L

Elm Bank Study Area
Below South Natick the Charles digresses to the north. It
is headed east to Charles River Village and thence to
Dedham, but first it takes a mitten-shaped detour. The
200-acre peninsula forming the mitten has been called
Elm Bank since 1740, when Colonel John Jones planted
elms along the Dover side of the river. Elm Bank was
acquired in 1874 by Benjamin Pierce Cheney, who made a
fortune in the express business and became the director
and largest shareholder of the American Express Company. Cheney built a summer home at Elm Bank which
was landscaped by the Olmsted brothers.
    Cheney's heirs gave Elm Bank to Dartmouth College.
In 1941, Dartmouth sold it to the Stigmatine Fathers who
built a classroom building and otherwise altered the
estate. In the 1960s the Commonwealth bought the property by mistake. The State College Board of Trustees con-
tracted for the purchase with the intention of siting the
Massachusetts College of Art at Elm Bank. By the time
they decided that the site was unsuitable they were
legally obliged to follow through on the purchase. The
property is currently managed by the Metropolitan District Commission for a mixture of uses including recreation. It is open to the public from 9 A.M. to dusk,
Wednesday through Sunday.

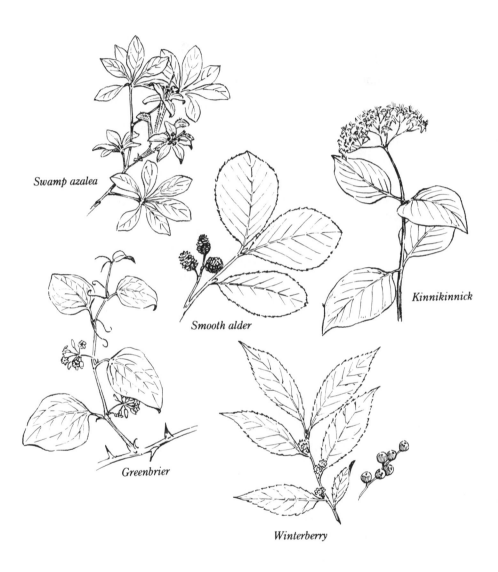

Swamp azalea

Smooth alder

Kinnikinnick

Greenbrier

Winterberry

Riverbank shrubs include swamp azalea, smooth alder, kinnikinnick, greenbrier, and winterberry. The most frequently seen is kinnikinnick, also called silky dogwood, which is described on page 117.

93

Because the well defined riverbank supports a nice variety of shrubs, this is a good place to learn some of them. Streamside flowering plants can be divided into four categories: trees, shrubs, vines, and herbaceous plants. Trees, shrubs and some vines have rigid (woody) structures that live year after year. Shrubs are distinguished from trees by their multiple trunks and lower height. Vines need the support of other plants to reach the sunlight. Herbaceous plants grow from the ground up every spring.

In summer canoeists can enjoy the sensuous flowers of the shrub *Rhododendron viscosum*, which is called by the common names clammy azalea, swamp honeysuckle, swamp pink, swamp azalea, and white azalea. Botanists usually stick to scientific nomenclature to avoid such confusion. Once it has been stated, the genus name is often abbreviated with its initial. *R. viscosum* has white or pink flowers with five petals. The base of the flower is a hairy, sticky tube that is longer than the petals. This attractive plant grows on moist, partially shaded sites from Maine to South Carolina. As suggested by the genus name it is closely related to rhododendron, but most rhododendrons are evergreen, while most azaleas, including *R. viscosum*, are deciduous. The tops of its leaves are glossy green. It is a branching shrub three to eight feet tall. As is typical of this genus, the leaves are in clusters attached to the tips of the twigs. In the leafless months the genus can be identified by the large flower bud at the end of many twigs.

Alder is another of the shrubs found at Elm Bank. Two shrub species are present here and elsewhere along the Charles: speckled alder and smooth alder. These are easily told from other shrubs at almost any season by the presence of the durable structures resembling miniature pine cones that held the plant's seeds. Botanists call them "fruiting strobiles." Though the strobiles make it easy to distinguish alders from other shrubs, telling speckled alder (*Alnus rugosa*) from smooth alder (*Alnus serrulata*) is sometimes a challenge. The leaves of speckled alder are widest at the middle, while smooth alder leaves are widest above the middle. An individual plant may not be true to either type, because there are variations in form within the species, and occasional hybrids.

The common wild grape at Elm Bank and elsewhere
on the riverbanks is fox grape, *Vitis labrusca.* The fruit of
wild grapes is edible, of course. It ripens in late summer
and early fall, and is easily collected from canoes where
vines overhang the river. Earlier in the season the young
leaves can be boiled lightly and used to wrap food for
baking. Concord and other commercial varieties of grapes
were developed from fox grapes. Wild grapes are sought
as food by birds such as grouse and doves, and by mammals including squirrels, skunks, and rabbits.

Greenbrier (*Smilax rotundifolia* and other species) is
another vine seen at Elm Bank. It is our only woody vine
with both thorns and tendrils. Its green stems form
dense, thorny tangles, but the thorns are straight and
therefore somewhat less troublesome to walkers than the
hooked thorns of blackberry and wild roses. The small,
light-green flowers of greenbrier appear in early summer
but are inconspicuous. Greenbrier is heavily browsed by
deer. Raggedy stem ends of this plant are a sign that deer
are present.

Riverbank shrubs, on the whole, do not make much of
an autumn display. An exception is winterberry, which is
at its prettiest in October, when its leaves form a golden
background for brilliant red-orange berries. In June winterberry puts out small white flowers attached directly to
the twigs. Female plants produce inedible stemless red
berries that stay on the plant long into the winter. Winterberry is also called black alder and winterberry holly; its
scientific name is *Ilex verticillata.*

Bays Region Study Area
Between Elm Bank and the Cochrane Dam, the valley of
the Charles provides a flat-bottomed corridor for the
river. Evidently the river's course on the floor of the
valley has shifted over the centuries, resulting in a series
of abandoned channels through which no current flows.
These upstream-pointing fingers of water are called back-
waters, sloughs, or bays. The lowermost of them, at the
area known as Charles River Village, is called Redwing
Bay. The others are without proper names. The bays are
set off from the river by low peninsulas. Because these
have so much "edge," where one plant group gives way to
another, the Bays Region forms a rich natural community.
It is an excellent place to see wetland plants, herons,
marsh wrens, and other birds.

The peninsulas are dominated by reed canarygrass, a perennial that makes good hay and grows in wet lowland meadows. Its flowers appear early in the summer, and remain above the leaves for the rest of the season. The seeds and leaves of this grass feed insects that in turn sustain fish, amphibians, and birds.

Along the fringes of reed canarygrass are emergent aquatic plants, those which are adapted to being rooted below the water, but whose leaves and flowers stand in the air above the surface. Emergent plants frequently seen along the Charles include three with arrowhead-shaped leaves: pickerelweed, arrow arum, and arrowhead. Though the three are similar in size and shape, they are easily distinguished by their flowers or by their leaf shapes and the patterns of veins within the leaves. Pickerelweed is the most common and most conspicuous of the group, because its violet flowers are visible for many weeks of the summer. Arrow arum blooms in late June and early July. The small flowers form a yellow stalk partially hidden within a green leaf-like envelope called a spathe. Arrowhead is the last to bloom. Its flowers appear on the flowerstalks in trios, and each has three white petals.

The marsh wren is a tiny champion of musical vitality.

In the warm, shallow water at the tips of the bays, a host of invertebrate animals thrive on a food chain based on the wetland plants. At the ends of some of the bays are muck-bottomed shallows dotted with yellow flowers. These are horned bladderworts. Bladderworts are carnivorous; their underwater leaves and stems have small

The yellow flowers of horned bladderworts are found in the warm shallow at the tips of the bays. The mayfly on the stem is one inch long.

bladders that rapidly expand when tiny animals, such as microscopic crustaceans, touch the hairs at the openings of the bladders. The animals are sucked into the bladder and digested.

Three kinds of herons are commonly seen along the Charles: great blue herons, black-crowned night herons, and green-backed herons. Any of these is likely to appear in the Bays Region, where the fertile biological community of the warm, shallow sloughs produces plenty of small fish, amphibians, and crayfish, which herons hunt. Standing as if caught in a game of freeze-tag, peering into the water, herons wait for a meal to swim to them. Sometimes they wade stealthily through the shallows or stalk along the shoreline, their eyes bright, steady, and sharp; their bills quick at the end of sinuous necks.

Great blue and black-crowned night herons nest in colonies. Great blue herons build nests in the tops of

97

trees killed by dams made by beavers or humans. Night herons nest on islands in Boston Harbor. They become more numerous on the Charles as the harbor is approached. Green-backed herons are the smallest of the three, and they are less gregarious in their nesting habits. Green-backed herons breed throughout the Charles Basin and are commonly seen at the edges of ponds and streams, as well as along the river itself.

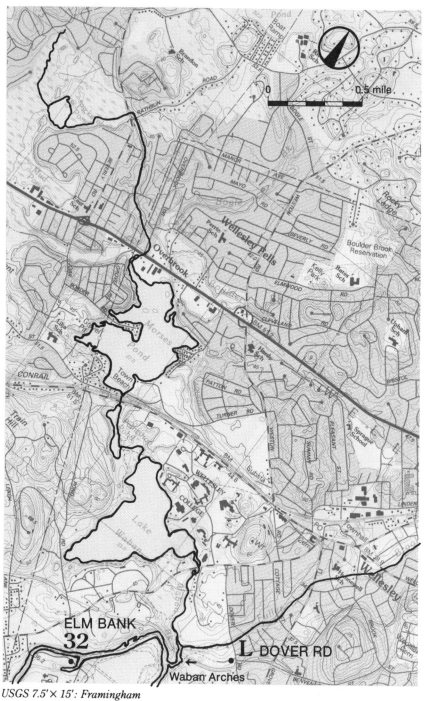

USGS 7.5' × 15': Framingham

Waban Brook/Charles River: Town of Wellesley

Tributary

Waban Brook

Access Points

Canoe

32 ELM BANK, Dover (mile 39.0)
USGS Framingham quadrangle
At present, this Metropolitan District Commission park is
open Wednesday through Sunday, from 9 A.M. to dusk.
The park is entered from Washington Street (Route 16)
in Wellesley. Cars cross the Charles on the narrow
Cheney Bridge, turn right onto the one-way road through
the property, and circle back nearly to the entrance
before reaching the canoe launch. The grass parking area
holds ten cars. Elm Bank offers excellent walking trails
along the Charles.

Foot

L DOVER ROAD, Wellesley
USGS Framingham quadrangle
Pedestrians atop the Sudbury Aqueduct get a nice view
from the Waban Arches and access to trails along the
river. Parking is difficult because there is no pulloff and
the shoulder is quite narrow near the aqueduct, but on-
road parking is possible a few hundred feet southeast of
the aqueduct.

See also: Access 32.

Comments

The combined waters of Fuller and Waban Brooks enter the
left side of the Charles at mile 39.4, opposite the end of the
north-thrusting peninsula called Elm Bank. The Waban
Arches overlook the confluence. These masonry arches bear
the Sudbury Aqueduct across the brook. Canoeists armed
with dip nets can salvage golf balls from the bottom of
Waban Brook; their source will be evident a short distance
upstream.

The outing suggested below ends at the junction of the
brooks, but strong paddlers can ascend Waban in high
water. The channel is narrow but deep. Canoeists can

expect to gain intimate familiarity with streamside vegetation, because they will have to push through it. Reaching Washington Street (Route 16) one-half mile above Waban Arches requires about thirty minutes of hard work. Upstream of Route 16 is a dam portaged on the stream's left. This is the approximate site of the dam built by the Indians at South Natick to power a sawmill. The pond above the dam, now Lake Waban, has been known as Sawmill Pond, Cunningham's Pond, and Bullard's Pond. At the time the Christian Indians settled Natick, one of Wellesley's first white settlers, Andrew Dewing, had a garrison house near the Charles River, probably near the Waban Arches.

Lake Waban borders the campus of Wellesley College, which was founded by Henry Fowle Durant of Hanover, New Hampshire. Durant was much affected by the death of his son at the age of eight. He and his wife Pauline Adeline Fowle Durant decided to found an institution devoted to the higher education of young women. They chose not to name it for themselves. Construction began in August, 1871. Wellesley College opened in September of 1875 with 300 students.

Suggested Outings

Canoe
— Visit Waban Arches and ascend the lowest section of Waban Brook.
Distance: 1.8 miles round trip
Portages: None
Parking: Access 32

Walks
— Explore trails in the area of the Waban Arches. Distance: variable
Parking: Access L

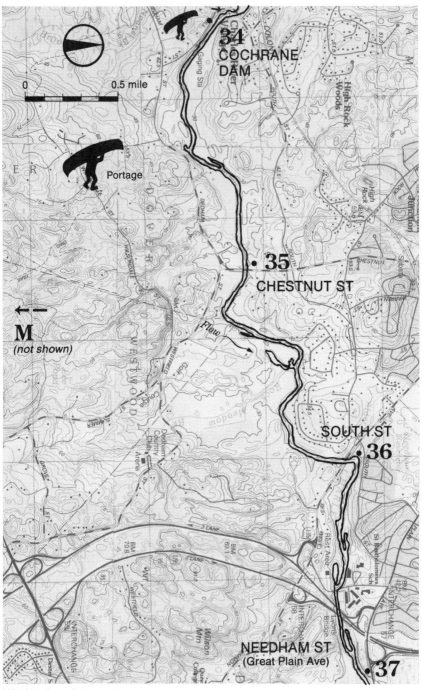

USGS 7.5′ × 15′: *Boston South, Framingham*

Charles River: Towns of Dedham, Dover, Needham, Westwood

Charles River Village

Access Points

Canoe

34 COCHRANE DAM, Dover (mile 44.5)
USGS Framingham quadrangle
To canoe downstream from Cochrane Dam, put in from
Mill Street, which parallels the right side of the river.
The best launch is about seventy-five yards below the
dam. Four cars can be parked along Mill Street.

35 CHESTNUT STREET, Needham and Dover (mile 45.9)
USGS Boston South quadrangle
The launch is now on the upstream left side of the
bridge, though that may change when the sewer con-
struction is completed. Three cars can be parked along
Chestnut Street.

36 SOUTH STREET, Needham (mile 47.5)
USGS Boston South quadrangle
This good point of access is near the intersection of
South Street and Route 135. The launch is on the left
bank at a sharp bend in the river. Six cars will fit in the
gravel parking lot.

37 NEEDHAM STREET, Dedham
GREAT PLAIN AVENUE, Needham (mile 48.9)
USGS Boston South quadrangle
A road barricaded against motor vehicles crosses the
Needham-Dedham boundary. It offers excellent access
from the left bank of the river. This area has served as
the starting line for canoe races on the Charles. Up to
three cars can be parked by the gate without blocking it.
Canoes can also be launched from pulloffs downstream
along Needham Street.

Foot

M HALE RESERVATION, Westwood
USGS Norwood quadrangle
Near but not on the banks of the Charles, Hale offers

extensive trails plus access to the contiguous Noanet Woodlands of The Trustees of Reservations. The entrance to Hale Reservation is at 80 Carby Street in Westwood. The office is open every day of the week.

Comments
Charles River Village is the neighborhood near the Cochrane Dam. There was a paper mill here in 1796, and throughout the 1800s this was a busy industrial village (see page 181). Upstream water was brought to a mill by way of a headrace that cut across the neck of a meander above the dam.

A Class II rapid is below the dam. It is short but it offers an opportunity for practicing white water techniques such as eddy turns, which paddlers use to enter sheltered places within a rapid. A slalom kayak course has been set up here. From wires stretched above the river, pairs of white poles are suspended to form gates that paddlers must navigate.

Soon after leaving the rapid, canoeists descending the Charles will arrive at the United States Geological Survey Gauging Station at mile 44.7. Here the river must pass over a sill and between abutments of concrete, through an opening of known dimensions. By measuring the level and speed of the water the discharge can be calculated. At this station the average discharge is 303 cubic feet per second. For comparison, the Assabet at Maynard discharges 187 cubic feet per second, as does the Sudbury as Saxonville. The average discharge of the Nashua River at East Pepperell is 573 cubic feet per second. The Mississippi's discharge is 640,000 cubic feet per second, or the equivalent of 2,100 Charles Rivers. The watershed of the Charles is 307 square miles, but the Mississippi drains 1,247,300 square miles.

Below the gauging station the channel is littered with boulders, which are submerged in high water. A straight reach of about a mile brings the canoeist to the steel and concrete bridge at Chestnut Street (Access 35). The current is fast at Chestnut Street, and canoeists should be alert for obstructions. In low water there are shallows at and below the bridge.

As the river turns sharply to the left, the town of Westwood has frontage on the Charles for a tenth of a mile. Dedham follows Westwood in possession of the right bank. On the right is the Dedham Country Club; Rock Meadow Brook flows through the golf course to the river. A residential area of Needham is on the left.

The bridge at Dedham Avenue is at mile 47.4. The abutments were placed in 1871 and an iron bridge was built, opening in 1873. The present bridge of two concrete arches was built in 1910 for $20,000. Access 36 is below the bridge, beside a wall of ledge. The compliant Charles turns sharply to the right and flows east for a mile to the handsome Lyons Bridge.

The first English settlers in this area lived in Dedham. They called the right bank near Lyons Bridge "The Canoes" because they kept boats here to ferry across to their fields at "The Great Plain," which became Needham. In the fields they grew corn, wheat, rye, and barley; vegetables were cultivated at home in kitchen gardens. In 1680 two men received permission to build a bridge at this location. For a long time it was called New Bridge. The Lyons Bridge was built in 1877 at a cost of $10,000, paid for by Dedham and Needham.

Below Lyons Bridge, Route 128 leaps the Charles at the first of its three intersections with the river. On a spring morning a phoebe singing here seemed to offer a philosophical commentary about traffic jammed on the highway overhead.

Access 37 is on the left, opposite a very steep right bank.

Suggested Outings

Canoe

Make the downstream run from South Street in Needham to the site of the Dedham Boat House.

USGS Boston South quadrangle
Distance: 4.6 miles
Parking:
  Upstream: Access 36
  Downstream: Access 38

Walks

— There is great walking at Hale Reservation, in Westwood, a short distance to the south of the Charles. Hale contains 1200 acres of woodlands and three ponds. It is contiguous with The Trustees of Reservations' 600-acre Noanet Woodlands. Trail maps are available at the office near the Hale Reservation entrance, Access M.

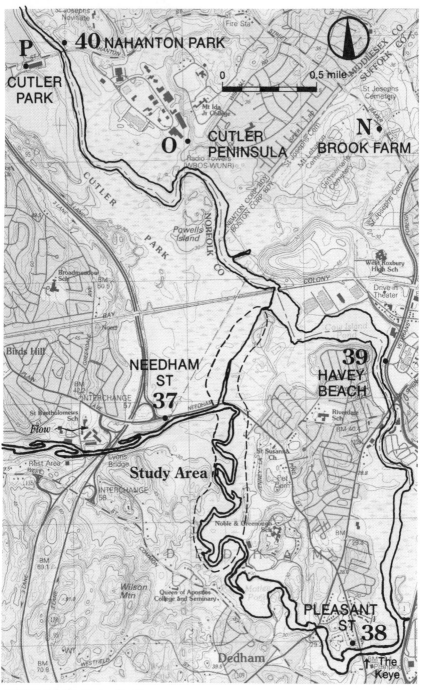

USGS 7.5' × 15': Boston South

Charles River: City of Newton, West Roxbury (City of Boston);
Towns of Dedham, Needham

Dedham Loop

Access Points

Canoe

37 NEEDHAM STREET, Dedham
GREAT PLAIN AVENUE, Needham (mile 48.9)
USGS Boston South quadrangle
A road barricaded against motor vehicles crosses the
Needham-Dedham boundary. It offers excellent access
from the left bank of the river. This area has served as
the starting line for canoe races on the Charles. Up to
three cars can be parked by the gate without blocking it.
Canoes can also be launched from pulloffs downstream
along Needham Street.

38 PLEASANT STREET, Dedham (mile 52.1)
USGS Boston South quadrangle
The launch is at the site of the Dedham Boat Club's boat
house. Six cars can be parked along Pleasant Street near
the Ames Street bridge.

39 HAVEY BEACH, Route 1, West Roxbury (mile 53.6)
USGS Boston South quadrangle
Havey Beach is on the right bank of the river. The beach
itself is now overgrown with alders and birches. The
brick bath house and concession buildings are still there,
but their windows are boarded up. Two cars can be
parked between them. There is more parking across the
Charles at Riverdale Park, but a sign there forbids the
launching of boats.

40 NAHANTON PARK, Newton (mile 56.7)
USGS Boston South quadrangle
Nahanton Park is on the Newton side near the Kendrick
Street bridge. At the river there is parking for twelve
cars and a small dock for launching canoes. Up the hill is
a second parking lot that will hold thirty cars.

Foot

N   BROOK FARM, West Roxbury
USGS Boston South quadrangle
The site of this transcendentalist community of the 1840s
is entered from Baker Street at the gate to Gethsemane
Cemetery. Three cars can be parked along the dirt road
that leads up the hill to the Eyrie and to Pulpit Rock.

O   CUTLER PENINSULA, Newton
USGS Boston South quadrangle
High ground at the end of this peninsula affords a broad
view of the Charles and its meadows when the trees are
without leaves. The trail, which is on public land, is
reached through a gate at the rear of a parking lot at a
GTE facility at the bend on Wells Avenue.

P   CUTLER PARK, Needham
USGS Boston South quadrangle
A 1.7-mile loop trail is entered through a gate at the cor-
ner of the parking lot of the GTE building on Kendrick
Street near the pond.

Comments

A sign at Access 37 marks the boundary between Needham
and Dedham. Upstream of this point Needham is to the
river's left and Dedham on the right. Downstream, both
banks are in Dedham. There is an impressive row of white
pines along the right bank.

The upstream opening of the Long Ditch is at mile 49.3.
The Long Ditch was dug in 1654 to reduce flooding of the
wet meadows and to reduce the damage to bridges from
high water. It is one-half mile long. At its passage under
Needham Street the water is shallow and an easy portage
may be necessary to enter. Below the bridge the Long Ditch
has a gentle current, and its traverse of the wide meadow
can be explored. This land is owned by the Metropolitan
District Commission, which calls the 700-acre tract Cutler
Park. It is included in the Natural Valley Storage Project,
protected by a flowage easement. Hunting is not permitted
here. The proportion of the Charles diverted into the ditch
varies with the water level. In high water more river takes
the short cut.

Below the mouth of the ditch the river begins a series of
meanders. It winds more than two miles from here to
Motley Pond, which is less than a mile away. Nature-
oriented canoeists will not mind, because this portion of the
Dedham Loop has much to savor. The banks are a mixture

of marsh and woodland with relatively little development. Visitors are surrounded by buttonbush, gray birch, maple, alders, willows, grape, elder, and river birch. Among the shrubs, kinnikinnick predominates. The community of streamside birds reflects the variety of the vegetation: great blue herons, black-crowned night herons, and green-backed herons all hunt here.

Noble and Greenough School is on the left bank at mile 51. Thomas Motley bought this property in 1851; his name adheres to the pond. A wealthy industrialist named Albert W. Nickerson purchased the land in 1883 and decided to build a castle on it. He hired architect Henry H. Richardson, and their creation was completed in 1890. The exterior is pink granite and brownstone from Delaware. Noble and Greenough School had been founded in 1866 to prepare students for entrance into Harvard. Its early quarters were in Boston. The school bought the Nickerson estate, called Riverdale, in 1921. Noble and Greenough students skate and row on Motley Pond, and in the summer a day camp launches boats and canoes here.

Bridge Street (Route 109) crosses at mile 50.9 on a beautiful three-arched bridge of unmortared granite in contrasting colors. Every piece has been cut to fit. A cart bridge was built at this site in 1642. Just above the cart bridge was a place where farmers washed their sheep before shearing, and where housewives retted their flax, which separated the filaments from the woody part of the plant. Flax fibers were made into linen cloth.

The bottom of the Dedham Loop is at Dedham Village, the center of this old town. The facilities of the Dedham Boat Club and the Dedham Canoe Club were on the left bank above Ames Street. The Dedham Boat Club built a boathouse here in 1875. The boathouse was torn down in 1935, and the land given to the Dedham Historical Society. The Dedham Canoe Club had an adjacent boathouse that continued in operation until the 1950s. On a high knob of granite overlooking this landing is a tiny brick building built in 1766, Dedham's powder house.

The founders of Dedham travelled up the Charles by boat, and landed at "the keye," which became Ames Street. Dedham's earliest river crossing was a ford here, followed by a footbridge. The Ames Street Bridge was built by Greenwood and Fuller in 1843 at a cost of $2,181. From beneath this bridge it can be seen that the original stone arch has been widened with concrete. This was done in 1926.

Beyond Ames Street the river is dominated by Route 1. The Dedham Mall and other large retail establishments come into view on the right, across the highway, as the Charles bends to the north. The diversion of Charles River water into Mother Brook is on the right at mile 52.4 (see page 180). On the average, a quarter of the river's flow is sent into the Neponset. Because of this diversion, the river's discharge into the Basin is the same as its discharge at Dover.

For a mile the channel proceeds straight down the middle of a wide marsh. At the end of this reach, near the mouth of a ditch at an automobile dealership, is a political boundary. Here, Norfolk County and Dedham meet Suffolk County and West Roxbury.

As the intersection of Routes 1 and 109 is approached, the banks are heavily developed. A big trailer park is near the right bank, followed by an apartment building. A boat dealership has a boat ramp on the left, upstream of Moseley's Dance Hall. A restaurant is on the left bank at mile 53.5, at the second Bridge Street (Route 109) bridge, which has five concrete arches. The Vine Rock Bridge, built about 1740, was an eighth of a mile downriver. It was replaced by a stone bridge at Bridge Street in 1828.

Beyond Bridge Street the atmosphere changes. On the left, Riverdale Park separates the river from a residential neighborhood. A playground and benches overlook the river, which is fringed with willows and silver maples. On the right is Havey Beach, which was a swimming beach operated by the Metropolitan District Commission. It is overgrown with alders. Though the water here is now usually clean enough for swimming, its natural murkiness does not meet modern water safety standards.

Across Route 1 from Havey Beach is a Veterans Administration hospital. Below the skating rink and swimming pool the Charles widens to become Cow Island Pond. At mile 54.5, where the Long Ditch rejoins the river, is a railroad bridge in use today for freight and commuter-rail service. What appears to be a large, treeless hill looms beyond the railroad bridge. This is the Gardner Street Landfill, the major Boston dump from the 1930s to the 1970s. Beneath thirty feet of refuse is Cow Island, which was a solitary hill opposite the lower end of the Long Ditch, north of the railroad. The mouth of Sawmill Brook is on the right bank past the landfill. From

1841 to 1849, this brook flowed through the Brook Farm Institute of Agriculture and Education, formed by George Ripley, a disaffected Unitarian minister. Cow Island was a favorite resort of young Brook Farmers. For more information about Brook Farm see page 175.

Two radio towers are on the right bank where the river makes an S-turn skirting Powell's Island. On the right is Cutler Peninsula, which can be reached from Access O on foot. The large red brick building on the right is the Wells Research Center. On the opposite bank, the meadow narrows. Where high ground reaches the river, one of the Cutler Park pathways does too, ending at a concrete barricade. Cutler Park is entered on foot at Access P.

The Nahanton Park canoe launch is below the Kendrick Street bridge on the right. Outcroppings of Roxbury conglomerate, also called pudding stone, are visible in the park.

Suggested Outings

Canoe
— Visit the Dedham Loop Study Area by launching at Dedham's Town Landing on Pleasant Street and canoeing upstream.
Distance: Variable
Portages: None
Parking: Access 38

— Paddle through Cutler Park. The slack current offers little resistance, the river is wide, and Nahanton Park has a small dock for canoeists. This is a good trip for beginners, unless it is windy.
Distance: Variable
Portages: None
Parking: Access 40

— Canoe downstream from South Street, Needham, through this section.
Distance: 9.2 miles
Upstream: Access 36
Downstream: Access 40
Parking:
    Upstream: Access 36
    Downstream: Access 40

— Explore Brook Farm. The West Roxbury Historical Society has a map and interpretive material about Brook Farm. To request information, write the society at 1961 Centre Street, West Roxbury, Massachusetts, 02132. The Reservations Division of the Metropolitan District Commission also can provide information.
Parking: Access N

— Hike the 1.7-mile loop at Cutler Park. There is a broad, flat trail on the dike around the pond.
Parking: Access P

Dedham Loop Study Area

Long Ditch
Though it has been there more than three centuries, the Long Ditch looks as fresh and trim as if it had been carefully installed last autumn. Its banks are bare dirt crowned with reed canarygrass. Hay from this big meadow served early Dedhamites as petroleum serves modern residents: it fueled their transportation. It also thatched the roofs of their houses. It was to improve the

Bigtooth aspens release their seeds in a cottony material that aids their dispersal by wind.

conditions for the growth and harvest of this hay that the meadows were ditched; rains formed large, durable puddles in the middle of the flat, low-lying fields.

Why has the Charles not rushed through and widened the Long Ditch, and abandoned its longer channel? It surely would have if there were an appreciable fall anywhere in the Dedham Loop, because running waters seek the steepest gradient. But the drop in these five miles of river is negligible. And the inlet at Needham Street has a stony bed, resistant to erosion. Most of the Charles takes the long way around. At moderate water levels about a fourth of the river goes through the Long Ditch.

A few trees are scattered along the ditch, including wonderful specimens of black willow, *Salix nigra*. Black willow flowers are catkins which appear in early spring. Black willow leaves are one to six inches long, narrow, and finely toothed. Sometimes this plant takes the form of a shrub, and sometimes it grows into a tree as tall as sixty feet.

Another tree found on the Long Ditch is bigtooth aspen, *Populus grandidenta*, which is usually found in groups. The small and medium sized individuals have smooth bark with a unique grayish-yellow color. The upper bark of mature trees is also this color, but the lower bark becomes darker and rougher. The leaves are two to six inches long. Because the leaf stalks are flat and flexible, leaves flutter in the breeze, giving the tree a shimmering appearance. Aspens found along the river vary in their characteristics because species within the poplar-aspen-cottonwood genus (*Populus*) often reproduce by sprout growth, and such offspring can have unusual leaves. As with other plants in the willow family, individual poplars are either male or female. The seeds are released in cottony material that slows their fall, thus increasing their dispersal by wind. Aspen wood is a major source of food for beavers.

Entangled among the grasses along the ditch are vines with flowers resembling morning glories. This is hedge bindweed, a native vine that blooms all summer. A pest to gardeners, bindweed gives pleasing variety to the grasses in the meadow. Plants of the genus *Rubus* grow beside the Long Ditch. *Rubus* includes the berry-producing canes: raspberries, dewberries, and blackberries.

Similarities within the genus confound easy identification, but riverside habitats are more hospitable to dewberries than to the others.

Dedham Meanders
Below the entrance to the Long Ditch the river takes a sharp right turn away from Needham Street and begins to writhe for the first time since Medfield. Road noise fades in these meanders. A particular tree is common here and nowhere else on the Charles: the river birch, *Betula nigra*. River birch is native to the southeastern United States, but has been successfully introduced to Massachusetts streamsides. It is easily identified by the raggedy pinkish-brown bark on the trunks of young trees and the upper parts of mature trees. River birch reaches

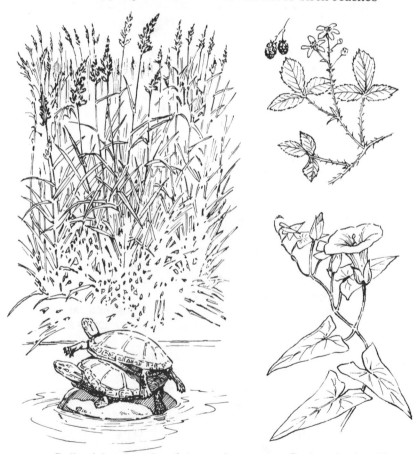

Dedham's broad meadows feature reed canarygrass. Dewberry is a bramble that grows in wet places. Bindweed is closely related to morning glory. When turtles outnumber basking sites, they improvise.

River birch, common in the meanders of the Dedham Loop, has raggedy, pinkish-brown bark.

up to fifty feet in height. The wood is useful for furniture and woodenware because it is strong and easily worked.

Gray birch, *Betula populifolia*, the other birch common along the Charles, is smaller and has wider distribution than river birch. A short-lived species, gray birch seldom grows taller than thirty feet and most of those along the river collapse before they are more than a few inches in diameter. Because its bark is white this tree is often confused with American white birch, the classic paper birch that provided Native Americans with bark for canoes. The bark of gray birch does not readily peel into layers, and its chalky color lacks the creaminess of the American white birch. The leaf of the gray birch has a long point.

Kinnikinnick (pictured on page 93) is the most common shrub along the Charles, and it dominates the banks in this study area. It is in the genus *Cornus*, the dogwoods. Kinnikinnick blooms in June in clusters of small off-white flowers. A month later the flowers have been replaced with clusters of fruit that ripens to blue.

Most are eaten by sparrows, gray catbirds, waxwings and other birds before the fall is very old. Dogwoods are such prolific producers of fruit that they are rated fifth among all woody North American plants for value to wildlife, behind pine, oak, blackberry, and cherry.

Kinnikinnick makes itself conspicuous in the leafless months by its maroon twigs. A close relative, red osier dogwood, has bright red twigs. Other names for kinnikinnick are silky cornel, swamp dogwood, silky dogwood, and pale dogwood. The scientific name is *Cornus amomum*; red osier dogwood is *Cornus obliqua*. The bark of these wetland dogwoods was included in a blend of tobacco and other leaves, called kinnikinnick, that was smoked by some Native American tribes.

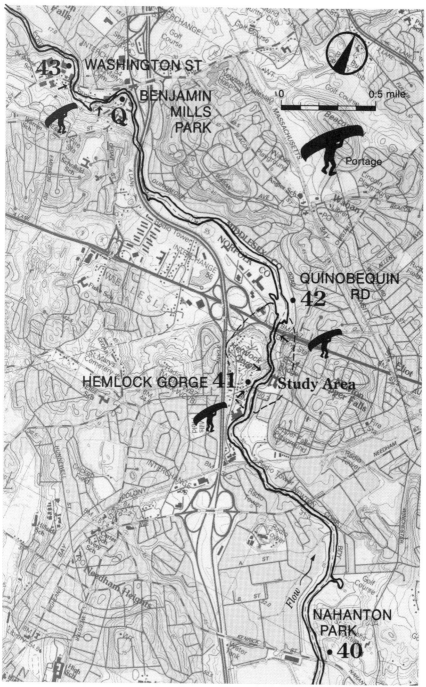

USGS 7.5'× 15': Boston South, Framingham

Charles River: City of Newton; Towns of Needham, Wellesley

Hemlock Gorge

Access Points

Canoe

40 NAHANTON PARK, Newton (mile 56.7)
USGS Boston South quadrangle
Nahanton Park is on the Newton side near the Kendrick Street bridge. At the river there is parking for twelve cars and a small dock for launching canoes. Up the hill is a second parking lot that will hold thirty cars.

41 HEMLOCK GORGE, Needham (mile 58.4)
USGS Boston South quadrangle
Parking is at Hamilton Place on the Needham side of the river. From Hamilton Place, canoes can be launched for paddling upstream. It is more practical to explore Hemlock Gorge on foot than by canoe. The Eliot Station of the MBTA Green Line is seven-tenths of a mile from Hemlock Gorge.

42 QUINOBEQUIN ROAD, Newton (mile 59.9)
USGS Boston South quadrangle
Quinobequin Road runs along the right side of the river from Upper Falls to Lower Falls. There are numerous pulloffs, and there are footpaths from the road to the river, as well as parallel to the river.

43 WASHINGTON STREET (Route 16), Wellesley (mile 60.9)
USGS Framingham quadrangle
Canoes can be launched from a parking lot behind the One Washington Street building, but this is private property and permission should be obtained to park here.

Foot

Q BENJAMIN MILLS PARK, Wellesley
USGS Framingham quadrangle
Benjamin Mills Park is reached from Water Street in Wellesley or from Quinobequin Road in Newton. Parking is as available at the Newton-Wellesley Industrial Park. A footbridge crosses the river at the park.

See also: Access 41 above.

Comments

Below Nahanton Park the Charles is wide and smooth. Gray birch and chokecherry line the banks. Several radio towers are visible ahead; antennas in this area are central to the metropolitan Boston market. There is a pretty stone railroad bridge at mile 57.4, on a spur line that carried ice to Boston from the pond at Cutler Park.

The concrete Highland Avenue-Needham Street bridge is reached at mile 57.6. Between here and Hemlock Gorge, land along the river banks is in a mixture of uses: industrial, commercial, and residential properties are visible. At mile 57.9 is a modern railroad bridge. Next to the concrete abutments, a set of stone abutments is visible. These were from the Charles River Branch of the Boston and Worcester Railroad, which was built in the 1850s to transport stone and gravel from Needham to fill Boston's Back Bay. At the peak of this activity, forty-car trains crossed this bridge once every forty-five minutes around the clock. By 1866 this line was part of the Woonsocket Division of the Boston, Hartford, and Erie Railroad.

The next bridge, three stone arches with wooden railings, is at mile 58.4. Here Elliot Street in Newton meets Needham's Central Avenue. Access 41 is on the left below the bridge. The Silk Mill Dam is downstream on the right; canoeists should take out well above the dam. The portage is on the left. There is a carry of 230 yards on the broad trail that leads down into the gorge between the falls and Echo Bridge.

Echo Bridge (mile 58.9) and the other features of Hemlock Gorge Reservation are described on page 124.

The Circular Dam (also called the Horseshoe Dam) is reached after a very short paddle. Canoeists should enter the channel on the right and take out at the end of it. The carry is 200 yards. Go beneath Route 9 on the Ellis Street underpass. Carefully cross the access road, then turn left onto the sidewalk that parallels the access road. Follow the sidewalk across the millrace to the opening in the guardrail. Descend the path leading to the river. This is Turtle Island. In 1803, when Turtle Island was the site of the Newton Iron Works, it was taken from Needham and annexed to Newton.

Before long, Route 128 appears on the left bank. Signs advertising upcoming exits for northbound drivers are visible from the water: "Grove Street MBTA station 3/4 mile." The Charles goes under Route 128 (for the second time) at mile 60.2. The Cochituate Aqueduct crosses a three-arched bridge below Route 128. This aqueduct was constructed in 1843 to transport water from Lake Cochituate, which was then called Long Pond. Water entered through a gate on the Wayland side of the lake and was carried to Chestnut Hill Reservoir in Boston.

Below the Water Street Bridge (mile 60.6) is the Cordingly Dam, which is portaged on the left. A carry of 150 yards is required to skirt the fish passage and the dam. The water is quick and shallow near the dam. Those wishing to reach slower, deeper water must carry another 150 yards through a parking lot.

For the history of Lower Falls, see page 182.

The Finlay Dam is reached almost immediately. Take out on the left and be careful crossing Washington Street (Route 16) which carries lots of traffic. Go to the left of the office building (One Washington Street), carry down the driveway, and launch from the parking lot at the rear of the building. Because this parking lot is private property, it may be necessary to obtain permission to use it.

Suggested Outings

Canoe
Canoeing this interesting section of the Charles requires four arduous portages around dams, with short paddles in between. Those determined to canoe the whole Charles will take the trouble, but others will find that recreational boating is more practical in other sections.

Walks
— Explore Hemlock Gorge Reservation.
Distance: Variable
Parking: Access 41

— Walk along the right bank of the river next to Quinobequin Road.
Distance: Variable.
Parking: Access 42

Hemlock Gorge Study Area
The place name "Upper Falls" refers to the short piece of the Charles between Elliot Street and Route 9. The falls have been "improved" with the construction of two dams, the Silk Mill Dam at the head of Hemlock Gorge, and the Circular Dam at the lower end of the gorge. There is only a quarter of a mile of river between the dams.

Echo Bridge has been a landmark at Hemlock Gorge since 1876.

The park is crossed by the Sudbury Aqueduct running from west to east, while the river flows here from south to north. The aqueduct passes high over the river on a masonry arch called Echo Bridge. There is a platform on the right riverbank, inside the base of the arch. A call from this platform creates an impressive string of echoes, a dozen or more audible repetitions. It is reported that a pistol shot echoes twenty-five times. Canoeists wishing to experiment should land a few feet downstream of the bridge. Echo Bridge was built in 1876 and 1877, at the same time as the Waban Arches, and for the same purpose: to carry the Sudbury Aqueduct across a low place. Echo Bridge is 500 feet long and has five arches in all. The span over the river is 130 feet long and rises 50 feet above the river.

Pedestrians can view the river from the top of the Echo Bridge. Looking upstream they see the complex of buildings preserved from manufacturing days. The high fall of water at the head of Hemlock Gorge offered an attractive supply of water power. In 1688 John Clark came here from Brookline and built a sawmill. His sons John and William added a fulling mill and a grist mill. In 1788 Simon Elliot bought part of the site and put in a snuff mill. By 1814 Elliot owned and operated four snuff mills, a grist mill, a wire mill, a screw factory, and a blacksmith shop, all powered by the river. By 1824 Upper Falls powered a large cotton mill. In 1886 the cotton mill was converted to spinning silk. The silk mill operated for many years, and the upper dam at Newton Upper Falls became known as the Silk Mill Dam. In 1964 the silk mill buildings were renovated and are now occupied by a restaurant with tables overlooking the river, antique stores, the New England School for Paperhanging, and several electronics businesses.

Downstream, a millrace forks to the left, forming an island of high ground beside the river. The canal supplies water to a reservoir lying alongside Route 9, which stored water for use in mills. The first was Jonathan Bixby's saw-mill in 1782. In 1792 the manufacturing of iron began at the Newton Iron Works, which rolled iron bars on Turtle Island (north of Route 9) for half a century. Nails were cut south of the street, and cotton cloth was made in a mill on the Needham side. The rolling mills were replaced by the Superior Wax Paper Company and other paper making concerns. The Worcester Turnpike opened for traffic in 1810. In 1834 the the opening of the Boston and Worcester Railroad doomed the turnpike, and it was soon abandoned as a toll road. The old turnpike has broadened into the present Route 9.

Hemlock Gorge is named for this attractive tree.

The deck of Echo Bridge is at treetop level; the crowns of mature white oak, white ash, and hemlock trees are passed while walking to the west end of the bridge. Down in the shady interior of Hemlock Gorge are exposures of bedrock. The stone is Roxbury conglomerate, also called pudding stone. Because conglomerate is obviously rocks within rock, it bears witness to the geologists' contention that the surface of our planet is subject to recycling by natural processes. The pebbles and cobbles within the conglomerate were rounded by the same agency that smooths chunks of rock today. Flowing water knocked them against each other often enough and long enough to remove every edge and corner. They were rounded by a river 600 million years ago, and then buried to a great depth under sediments that fell to the floor of an ancient sea. The combination of time, temperature, pressure, and chemistry resulted in the embedding of the stones within a matrix of finer sediment. In the course of many millions of years the fragment of Earth's crust bearing Roxbury conglomerate was pushed to the surface, exposed by erosion, and plastered onto the side of North America. So firmly are the pebbles joined to the matrix that Roxbury conglomerate has been cut and used as building stone.

Poison ivy grows as a creeper, as a small shrub, or as a tree-climbing vine.

From the safety of the trails at Hemlock Gorge those who have never had the opportunity to do so can learn to identify poison ivy, which grows as a low trailing vine at the base of the shaded ledges. People who want to explore the outdoors in southern New England need to know what poison ivy looks like so they can evaluate how much exposure can be risked without developing an annoying, long-lasting rash. Human skin has an allergic reaction to the sap of this plant, but individual sensitivities differ widely.

Poison ivy leaves are grouped in threes, and its veins and stems are reddish where the leaves join. Poison ivy is a kind of sumac that grows as a creeper, as a small shrub, or as a tree-climbing vine. Poison oak is a close relative that prefers drier sites and latitudes lower than New England's. Some scientists think that poison oak and poison ivy are varieties of the same species; for practical purposes they are indistinguishable. Poison ivy likes plenty of moisture and partial or heavy shade. Only human beings are allergic to this plant. Deer eat it, and the folklore has it that the milk of a poison-ivy-eating nanny goat reduces the vulnerability of those most allergic to it. For the majority of canoeists, long pants are sufficient protection against occasional exposure to poison ivy during portages.

Another plant associated with the ledges of conglomerate at Hemlock Gorge is a pretty evergreen fern named polypody that finds footholds in the stone. Its ability to survive with so little soil gains polypody a niche where other plants are unable to crowd it out.

It is pleasing to find Hemlock Gorge well provided with hemlock trees, a flat-needled conifer native to Massachusetts forests. Stands of hemlocks scattered among deciduous woods shelter animals from severe weather. In winters when the snow is deep, groups of white-tailed deer take up residence in hemlock groves and leave many signs of their occupation: scats, buck rubs, and beds. Though the area around Hemlock Gorge is too urban for deer, the hemlocks upriver at Rocky Narrows sometimes shelter a herd of white-tails, the Charles River Basin's largest wild mammals.

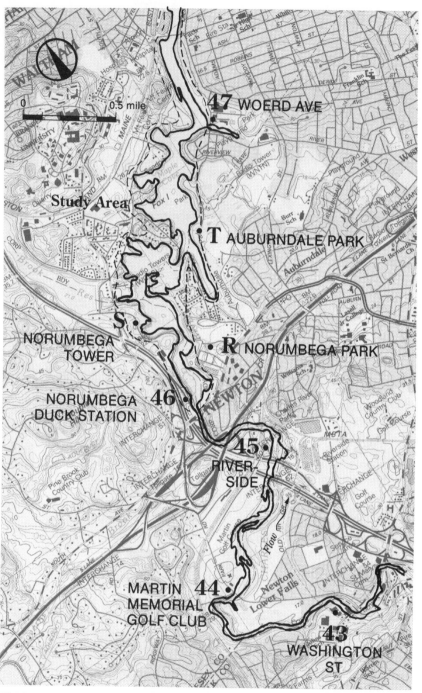

USGS 7.5′ × 15′: Boston South, Framingham

Charles River: Cities of Newton, Waltham;
Towns of Wellesley, Weston

Lakes
District

Access Points

Canoe

43 WASHINGTON STREET (Route 16), Wellesley (mile 60.9)
USGS Framingham quadrangle
Canoes can be launched from a parking lot behind the One Washington Street building, but this is private property and permission should be obtained to park here.

44 MARTIN MEMORIAL GOLF CLUB, Weston (mile 62.1)
USGS Framingham quadrangle
The entrance is from Park Road in Weston. The parking lot accommodates hundreds of cars, but at times it is filled, and improperly parked cars are towed. There is no official launch, but there is a nice place to put in beneath the trees near the parking lot.

45 RIVERSIDE, Weston (mile 62.9)
USGS Framingham quadrangle
Riverside is reached by way of Recreation Road, which intersects with Park Road at the boundary of the Martin Golf Club. The capacity of the parking lot is fourteen cars. Riverside Park has two footbridges over the Charles, and picnic tables.

46 NORUMBEGA DUCK FEEDING STATION, Weston; CHARLES RIVER CANOE AND KAYAK SERVICE, Newton (mile 63.5)
USGS Framingham quadrangle
The Norumbega Duck Feeding Station, which is also the parking area for the Charles River Canoe and Kayak Service, is reached by crossing the river westbound on Commonwealth Avenue (Route 30), turning right onto the northbound Route 128 access road, then immediately

bearing right onto Recreation Road. There is a large parking lot. Canoes can be launched from the duck feeding station, or rented from the canoe and kayak service. Paddling instruction is also available.

47 WOERD AVENUE, Waltham (mile 65.9)
USGS Boston South quadrangle
This public boat launch has a parking lot for several dozen cars and concrete and gravel boat ramps.

Foot

R NORUMBEGA PARK, Newton
USGS Framingham quadrangle
Norumbega Park is entered from the end of Woodbine Street. Six cars can be parked along the street.

S NORUMBEGA TOWER, Weston
USGS Framingham quadrangle
Eben Horsford's stone tower is on Norumbega Road. Ten cars can be parked along the road. From the tower walkers can reach paths along the wooded shore of the Charles.

T AUBURNDALE PARK
USGS Framingham quadrangle
From a large parking lot at the end of West Pine Street walkers can enjoy both Auburndale Park and the Forest Grove Reservation.

See also: Access 45.

Comments
People fish from the shore behind One Washington Street and catch some big bullheads. The river is pretty and quiet. Lower Falls Park is on the right bank, wooded in some spots, marshy in others. The left bank is drier, supporting beech and other large trees. At mile 61.6, the Wellesley-Weston boundary is passed.

The bridge at mile 62.0 connects Park Road on the Weston side with Newton's Concord Street. Canoe access from the parking lot of the Metropolitan Distric Commission's Martin Golf Course is sixty yards below the bridge on the left.

Swamp loosestrife, pickerelweed, yellow pond lily, and arrowwood are found in the marshy stretch between the golf course and Route 128. Near the highway, big aspens disperse their cotton-like fruits in mid-June, and at times the surface of the water is snowy with them. Wild roses grow between the lanes of Route 128. This is the third and final crossing of the Charles by that traffic artery. The highway is beside the river for another mile.

The area east of Route 128 is called Riverside. There was a private recreation facility by that name on the Weston side of the river, the Riverside Recreation Grounds, which opened in 1898. It had a variety of athletic facilities as well as a restaurant and boat houses. It was connected to the Riverside Depot of the Boston and Albany Railroad by foot-bridges, which remain part of the park.

The Boston and Albany Railroad evolved from the Boston and Worcester Railroad of the 1830s. Though its ownership has passed through many corporations, this line is still Boston's major rail route to the west. Today it carries Amtrak and Conrail through trains, and commuter service that extends to Framingham. Riverside Depot has become the terminal station on the Green Line, which provides electric trolley service to downtown Boston.

Below Riverside the Charles is dominated by curving ramps and broad ribbons of concrete. This highway interchange links Route 128, the Massachusetts Turnpike, and Route 30. Because runoff from the highways is not filtered by soil and vegetation, salt and oil enter the river.

Once past Commonwealth Avenue (Route 30) at mile 63.4, canoeists enter the area known as Norumbega, at the head of the Lakes District. The Norumbega Duck Feeding Station is on the left. On the right an old Metropolitan District Commission police station has been leased to the Charles River Canoe and Kayak Service, which rents boats and gives instruction in their use. Next door is the headquarters of the Charles River Watershed Association. During business hours the public is welcome to stop in; information about the river is available here, and many old photographs of the Charles adorn the walls. Across the cove is a Marriott Hotel. For more information about this area, see "Lakes District Study Area" below.

At mile 64.2, next to several radio towers, is the mouth of Stony Brook, which marks the boundary between Weston and Waltham. Much Stony Brook water never reaches the Charles because it is diverted for the municipal water supply of the City of Cambridge. Norumbega Tower is on the Weston side (see page 135). Below Stony Brook the river squeezes between arms of high ground. Auburndale Park lies alongside "Pulsifer's Cove," formed by the neck of land on the right. This inlet is also called Purgatory Cove, an ironic reference to its use for baptisms. Below this park, both banks of the river are part of Waltham. On the left bank are Sandy Nook and Maple Cove. The Woerd Avenue boat launch is on the right. Woerd rhymes with bard, which means pronunciation varies according to the accent of the speaker.

Suggested Outings

Canoe
— Explore the Lakes District. Courtship canoeing is a tradition here. Canoes can be rented here from the Charles River Canoe and Kayak Service.
Distance: Variable
Portages: None
Parking: Access 46

— Make the downstream run from Martin Golf Course to the Woerd Avenue boat launch.
Distance: 3.8 miles
Portages: None
Parking:
    Upstream: Access 44
    Downstream: Access 47

Canoeing at the Lakes District about 1900.

Walks
— Hike around the Lakes District. Pedestrians can cross
the river at Commonwealth Avenue and Prospect Street,
and can stay at or near the riverbank for most of the
journey.
Distance: 4.7 miles
Parking: Access R or any other Lakes District
access point

Lakes District Study Area
The office of the Charles River Watershed Association is
at the water's edge in the Lakes District. The Association
was established in 1965. Its staff works to protect the
river environment, to maximize public access to the
Charles, and to promote its recreational use. It is a tax-
exempt organization supported by its members. For
membership information contact: Charles River
Watershed Association, 2391 Commonwealth Avenue,
Auburndale, Massachusetts, 02166.

A picturesque boathouse first built for waterborne
police now houses the Charles River Canoe and Kayak
Service. The building it occupies remains from a period in
which the Charles River was the site of many social and
recreational activities, and the Lakes District was a focal
point because the Basin had not yet been constructed.

> Occasionally in September, a spectacle is presented here
> that not even Venice in her palmiest days could have far
> surpassed. On an appointed night the steamer "White
> Swan" starts up river from Waltham, followed by upwards
> of 400 boats, of every variety, from leaky yawls and crazy
> rafts to costly cedar shells and aboriginal canoes, and the
> kerosene steamers of the newspaper reporters. Every
> boat is belted with lines of lanterns, and filled with joyous
> monarchs of the wave; and from sundry islands and
> moored rafts, salvos of artillery, rockets, golden rain,
> Japanese fires, fiery colored stars, and other pyrotechnics
> flame across the black sky, while the great estates along
> the shores and the railroad and corporation properties are
> brilliantly illuminated. On the river there are thousands of
> people, with myriads on the shores; and the music of
> military bands is taken up from point after point, as the
> magnificent *cortege* moves up to Fox Island and Islington,
> following the White Swan as its Bucentaur, Newton Boat
> Club, Boston Canoe Club, Arlington Canoe Club, Somer-
> ville Boat Club, Waltham Canoe Club, Upper-Charles-
> River Boat Club, Aurora Canoe Club, Harvard Club, and
> others, each with from a dozen to fifty boats in massed
> column, their oars and paddles keeping time to the sweet

music of the bands and the choruses of the rowers, whose
charming boat-songs reverberate from the forested banks
and the island thickets.

(from *King's Handbook of Newton*
by M.F. Sweetser, 1889)

The Lakes District came into being after the enlarge-
ment of Waltham's Moody Street Dam in 1814, which
deepened the water of the previous mill pond. The Boston and Worcester Railroad gave Bostonians access to
boating on this placid part of the Charles. Later, the electric street railroad along Commonwealth Avenue provided transportation directly to the Lakes District.
Bostonians were drawn up the Charles because it was
still tidal at Boston and unsuitable for recreation; the
Basin did not exist until the construction of the Charles
River Dam, completed in 1910.

Boating for pleasure became very fashionable toward
the end of the nineteenth century and in the early years
of the twentieth. At the beginning of this period the mass
production of wood and canvas canoes was perfected, and
two of the manufacturers, Robertson and Partelow, had
factories near the Lakes District. The manufacturers,
hotels, and private clubs all maintained boat houses from
which canoes could be rented, or in which those who
owned canoes could store them, a necessary service in
the days before automobiles. Such boat houses stood
along the Charles wherever rail transportation made it
possible for urbanites to reach them: above Upper Falls in
Newton, at Bridge Street in West Roxbury, in Dedham at
Ames Street, in South Natick, in Medfield at Route 109,
and at the pond above the West Medway Dam. But the
greatest concentration of boathouses was in the Lakes
District.

Photographs from the turn of the century show large
numbers of canoes, often with a pair of young adults in
each, the young man seated in the stern under a straw
skimmer, paddle in hand. The lady sat facing him on
cushions at the bottom of the boat, holding an open book
and a parasol. Today's approach to pleasure boating
seems spartan in comparison.

Across a bay from the Charles River Canoe and Kayak
Service is a large Marriott Hotel that was built on part of
the site of Norumbega Park. The owners of the Commonwealth Avenue Street Railway developed Norumbega

Park in 1897 as an attraction to its western terminus.

In 1889 a stone tower was erected on high ground on the Weston side of the Lakes District, at the expense of Eben N. Horsford, who had formed the conviction that Vikings had settled here long before the English arrived. The inscription on the front of the tower makes these assertions: "Fort at base of tower and region about was occupied by the Breton French in the 15th, 16th, and 17th Centuries. River the Charles explored by Thorwald, Leif's Brother 1003 AD, colonized by Thorfinn Karlsefeni 1007 AD." Horsford's evidence for these claims is dismissed by modern scholars, but there is something attractive in his enthusiasm.

Horsford's stone tower can be considered a monument to imaginative speculation about the past. The tower is open to visitors. Inside, a spiral staircase winds around a column of cut granite cylinders. The stone stairs get some daylight from the windows. The wall is a colorful blend of miscellaneous fieldstone. From the top of the tower the river is visible to the south in the months when the oak trees are leafless.

The rise of the automobile dealt the Lakes District a triple blow. Automobiles gave young couples the same opportunities for privacy as canoes, with less risk of capsizing. Relieved of dependence on rail transportation, people chose from a wider menu of recreational locales, and since canoes can be carried on cars, boathouses lost their importance. Lastly, the construction of the superhighways reduced the attractiveness of the area.

The Lakes District offers good fishing. Large-mouthed bass are its most sought-after gamefish.

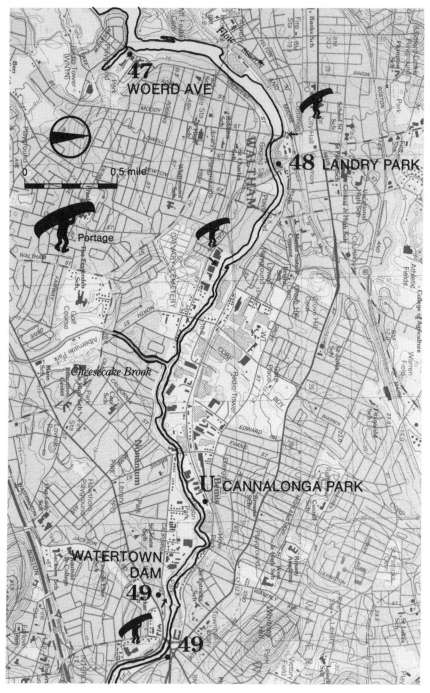

USGS 7.5'× 15': *Boston South*

Charles River: Cities of Newton, Waltham; Town of Watertown

Industrial Corridor

Access Points

Canoe

47 WOERD AVENUE, Waltham (mile 65.9)
USGS Boston South quadrangle
This public boat launch has a parking lot for several dozen
cars and concrete and gravel boat ramps.

48 LANDRY PARK, Waltham (mile 66.3)
USGS Boston South quadrangle
Landry Park, on the left bank below the Moody Street Dam,
offers good canoe launches for downstream access. Parking
is in the city parking lot across the river, which is reached
from Cooper Street.

49 WATERTOWN DAM, Watertown (mile 69.3)
USGS Boston South quadrangle
Two-hour parking is permitted on California Street, which
parallels the narrow park on the right bank, upstream of the
dam.

Foot

U CANNALONGA PARK, Watertown
USGS Boston South quadrangle
This park has a large parking lot, picnic tables, and nice
views of the river. It overlooks the Bemis-Aetna Mills.

Comments

An enormous brick edifice is on the right bank downstream
of the Woerd Avenue boat launch. This was the famous
Waltham Watch Factory, built in the 1850s. The building is
narrow so that natural light can enter from both sides of the
work space. For additional information about Waltham's
industrial history, see page 177. On the left is Mount
Feake Cemetery. Prospect Street crosses at mile 65.8 on
three arches of gray stone. On the upstream left side of

this bridge is the foundation of a former riverfront dance-hall, Nuttings on the Charles.

The large industrial building to the left below the bridge houses Nova Biomedical. The oxidized copper church steeple on the left stands atop Waltham's First Congregational Church. Riverwalk Park is being constructed along the left bank, between the railroad and the Charles. The railroad was built in the 1840s as the Fitchburg Railroad. In *Walden*, Thoreau commented on the sound of its trains passing near Walden Pond.

Railroads played a major role in industrial development along the Charles River.

The Moody Street Bridge is nine arches of concrete just above the dam, which was built of granite in 1850. Canoeists should take out on the left bank above the bridge because the dock on the opposite bank is in poor condition. Across Moody Street are the big mill buildings of the Boston Manufacturing Company, now converted to housing for the elderly and other uses. In Landry Park, which is between the mills and the river, there are several places to put in. The Charles River Museum of Industry is in the powerhouse of the Boston Manufacturing Company at the downstream end of the mill complex. The museum has displays of textile, automobile, and clock manufacturing. It is open on Thursdays and Saturdays.

The United States Geological Survey monitors the quantity of water passing through the river 800 feet below Moody Street. The average discharge is 303 cubic feet per second. The average flow is exactly the same here as it is at Dover, twelve miles upriver, which suggests that the diversion at Mother Brook is made up by tributaries below Dedham.

There is a footbridge in Landry Park, then a railroad bridge supported by creosoted poles. At the Elm Street bridge (mile 66.5), the current is fast, and the riverbed is littered with rocks and shopping carts. The pace slows at Newton Street (mile 66.7), which crosses on a bridge of three stone arches. There are white water lilies in pockets of slow water and trees on both sides of the river.

At mile 67.0 is another railroad bridge followed by another footbridge. At the Bleachery Dam (mile 67.3), the old headrace splits from the channel to the left. Take out on the right just above the dam, near the forest of telephone poles. There is a carry of 135 yards through this ghostly grove. Watch for shopping carts and boulders in the fast water below this dam.

Farwell Street is at mile 67.6, its bridge a single arch of concrete. There is fast water below the bridge, and many tires in the riverbed. Beyond Farwell Street, Watertown is on the left and Newton is again in possession of the right bank. The current slackens and big sycamore, catalpa, and elm trees grace the left bank. At mile 67.9, the mouth of Cheesecake Brook is on the right. Silver maples line both sides.

Cannalonga Park is on the left above Bemis. The Bemis Dam (mile 68.5) has a rich history. In 1760 David Bemis built a dam and mill at Bridge Street. Bemis made paper here beginning in 1779. When the paper mill burned in 1792, the General Court paid to rebuild it. In 1796, David's son Seth began making chocolate on the Watertown side. In 1803 he devised a way to manufacture cotton thread, and, later in the decade, other cotton products. Seth Bemis built a gas plant in 1812 for illumination in his mills. In the early 1820s the Boston Manufacturing Company, which operated the new cotton mill in Waltham, offered Bemis one thousand dollars for every inch he would agree to lower his dam. He lowered it twelve inches and installed a novel "rolling" dam, which is usually referred to as the "rolling stone dam." The dam itself was a cylinder mounted on an axle. By rolling the cylinder on the inclined plane beneath it, the water level could be adjusted.

The Aetna Company's textile mills are on the left, and the millrace and the old brick Bemis building are on the right. After 1860 the Aetna Company made woolen textiles in mill buildings on both sides of the river. The power of the two water wheels was connected with a belt of cable so that either mill could employ the power of both wheels. Aetna sold the property in 1934. The dam was breached about 1944, leaving a riffle that can be run in times of moderate flow. If the water is too low a long carry around the mill buildings is necessary. Canoes can be landed on either bank, but must be launched below Bridge Street from the left bank. Below Bemis the right bank has a residential flavor — decks shaded by weeping willows overlook the river. The left bank is lined with commercial and industrial property.

Allison Park (a group of playing fields) is on the right bank at mile 68.8, and Watertown's Pleasant Street passes near the left bank at mile 69.0. A small island divides the channel as the river enters an S-curve here. At the end of the reach below this curve, Watertown leaps the river and takes possession of both banks for one-half mile. This land was set apart from Newton to make sure that Watertown continued to benefit from uncontested ownership of the prime fish harvesting zone at its falls.

The takeout is just below the Thompson Footbridge, in the park on the right bank.

Suggested Outings

Walks

— Visit the Charles River Museum of Industry, which is open Thursdays and Saturdays. Park at Access 47.

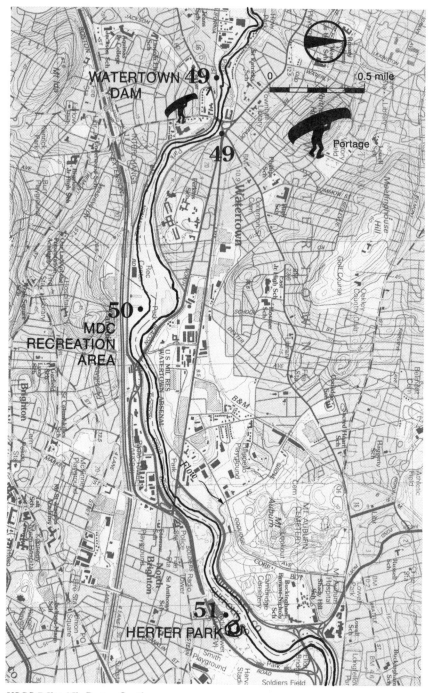

USGS 7.5' × 15': Boston South

Charles River: Brighton (City of Boston),
Cities of Cambridge, Newton; Town of Watertown

Upper
Basin

Access Points

Canoe

49 WATERTOWN DAM, Watertown (mile 69.3)
USGS Boston South quadrangle
Two-hour parking is permitted on California Street, and
canoes can be put in from the right bank. Below the dam,
parking is permitted along Charles River Road, which
runs along the left bank below Watertown Square.
Canoes can be launched from several points in the
narrow riverside park, which also provides good pedestrian access.

50 MDC RECREATION AREA, Brighton (Boston)
(mile 70.6)
USGS Boston South quadrangle
On Nonantum Road where Brighton bounds Newton,
there are two public parking lots at the river's edge, one
of which has a concrete boat ramp.

51 HERTER PARK, Allston (Boston) (mile 72.4)
USGS Boston South quadrangle
Herter Park is on the right bank, between the Charles
and Soldiers Field Road. It has a large parking lot, and
canoes are easily launched from its manicured riverbank.

Foot

See Access 49.

Comments
Below the Watertown Dam the river is very shallow. Before
the mouth of the Charles was dammed, the falls here were
the head of the tidal estuary.

A single ninety-foot arch of stone and concrete suffices
to span the river at Watertown Square. This bridge, built
in 1905, was designed by Wilbur Learned, Watertown's
engineer. It is faced with granite cut in Deer Isle, Maine.

To this point the Charles retains its character as a small
river. The trees and shrubs are familiar to canoeists from

upriver: kinnikinnick, silver maple, oaks, and gray and river birch. Norway maples have been added to the riverside by civilization.

The Perkins School for the Blind, which is to the river's left, moved to Watertown from South Boston in 1912, purchasing a thirty-four acre estate. The school had been founded in 1829 by Dr. John Fisher with the help of a blind historian named William Prescott and a merchant, Thomas Handasyd Perkins, who had made a fortune in the China trade. Because of financial support provided by Perkins, the school was named after him. The huge tower of the main building is a landmark on this part of the Charles. There are many white water lilies on the edge of the river at the Perkins School.

Below Watertown, heavily travelled roads are near both sides of the Charles. Sometimes they are screened from view by a narrow strip of trees, but at other times the traffic is in sight from the river. The Newton Yacht Club is on the right at mile 70.3. Boston's tallest skyscrapers come into view here.

The Watertown Yacht Club is behind an island on the left bank. On the right bank, opposite the island, is the boundary between Newton and Boston. Access 50 is on the right bank at a public recreation center, where a concrete boat ramp provides access for trailered boats. Riverside trees are willow, chokecherry, silver maple, and river birch.

The North Beacon Street (Route 20) Bridge is three arches of concrete. On the left is the Watertown Arsenal, where fifty Indians camped during the siege of Boston at the beginning of the American Revolution. The federal government chose this as an arsenal site in 1816. It manufactured cartridges and gun mounts before the Civil War, and during that war it became a foundry and metals-testing center. During World War I shells were made here, and during World War II, antiaircraft guns, howitzers, and mortars. Much of the arsenal was sold to the city of Watertown in 1968.

The black-crowned night heron presents itself as the avian symbol of the lower Charles. Individual herons stand in the shallow water at frequent intervals, red-eyed, remarkably tame. In some places on midsummer afternoons a dozen can be seen in a glance, one bird every ten yards. They never stand in groups.

*In summer, black-crowned night herons are numerous
along the Upper Basin.*

The Arsenal Street Bridge is two spans of concrete, with its facade crumbling. There is a little marsh on the left bank, with phragmites, bindweed, elder, and kinnikinnick.

Not far to the river's left is Mt. Auburn Cemetery, which was founded in the 1831 as an innovative combination of rural cemetery and horticultural garden. It is now famous for attracting migrating warblers. Cambridge Cemetery is between Mt. Auburn and the Charles.

On the right just above Herter Park is the new Northeastern University Boat House. The interest in rowing at Northeastern and other schools spawned the Head of the Charles Regatta. Thousands of rowers from over 250 colleges and athletic clubs participate in the three mile race, and over 150,000 spectators crowd on bridges and along the banks. Racers compete in thirty-two categories in what is said to be the largest single-day rowing event in the world.

Herter Park, Access 51, has a playground at its upstream end.

Suggested Outings

Canoe

— From Herter Park, paddle upstream to Watertown Dam and back.
Distance: 5.4 miles round trip
Portages: None
Parking: Access 51

— Canoe downstream from the Watertown Dam to Captain's Island.
Distance: 5.5 miles
Portages: None
Parking:
    Upstream: Access 49
    Downstream: Access 52

Walks

— Walk along the left bank of the Charles from Watertown Square to Beacon Street and back.
Distance: 2.8 miles round trip
Parking: Access 49

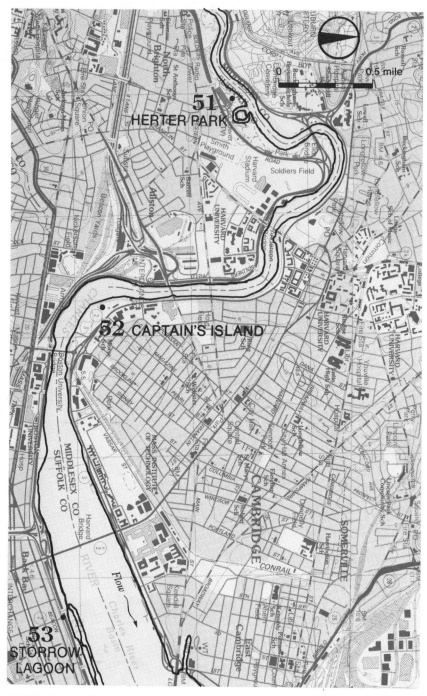

USGS 7.5′× 15′: Boston South

Charles River: Allston, Brighton (City of Boston);
City of Cambridge

Middle Basin

Access Points

Canoe

51 HERTER PARK, Allston (Boston) (mile 72.4)
USGS Boston South quadrangle
Herter Park is on the right bank, between the Charles and Soldiers Field Road. It has a large parking lot, and canoes are easily launched from its manicured riverbank.

52 CAPTAIN'S ISLAND, Cambridge (mile 74.8)
USGS Boston South quadrangle
Twenty-five cars can be parked in the lot near the swimming pool at Magazine Beach.

53 STORROW LAGOON, Boston (mile 76.6)
USGS Boston South quadrangle
Though most canoe landings must have automobile parking to qualify as access points, allowances must be made for downtown Boston. The Esplanade has easy launching in its sheltered lagoons.

Foot
Both shores of the Charles River Basin are open to pedestrian use.

Comments

At Herter Park an outdoor theater is surrounded by a moat of Charles River water.

The riverbanks are lined with gray birch, chokecherry, and, if it is summer, black-crowned night herons. On the water are cormorants, and, depending on the weather and the day of the week, boats. Rowers in their fast-moving shells are impatient with canoeists who block their paths. Canoeists face forward, and the more leisurely pace of their sport leaves them time to show consideration. They should give rowers plenty of room.

The Eliot Bridge (mile 72.9) is brick with light gray stone trim. It was built in 1951. On the left bank is "Gerry's Landing," where in 1630 Sir Richard Saltonstall's party arrived to establish Watertown (see page 176). The poet James Russell Lowell lived here and praised the beauty of the salt marshes which then spread to the south. There was a bathing beach here until about 1950, when construction began for the Eliot Bridge.

The river bends to the right, and the Prudential Tower becomes visible again. The red building is Harvard's Newell Boat House, on a site previously occupied by a coal and lumber yard. Below the Harvard Boat House is the Anderson Bridge, which replaced the Boylston Street drawbridge in 1913. Cambridge's first bridge, the "Great Bridge," was built here in 1660-1662. It was approached on causeways through broad marshes, which have been filled. The materials of the Anderson Bridge, brick and concrete, were chosen to harmonize with the Weld Boat House on the left bank below the bridge. On the right is Harvard Stadium, one of the first reinforced-concrete structures in the world when it was built in 1903. The buildings of Harvard are in sight on both sides of the river, and several of those on the left have colorful cupolas. Eliot House wears a turquoise crown; that of Dunster House is crimson. The handsome John W. Weeks Footbridge allows pedestrians to cross from one Harvard campus to the other. The Harvard Business School was built on the south bank in 1926 and 1927, and the Weeks Bridge erected at the same time.

During warm weather people relax in the sun on both sides of the river, reading, sunbathing, and exercising, their view of the Basin unobstructed from either Boston or Cambridge.

Western Avenue crosses the Charles at mile 74.3 on three shabby concrete arches, and River Street a fifth of a mile below. On the right, the Guest Quarters Suite Hotel stands out. The Polaroid Building is on the Cambridge bank at mile 74.6 near the end of this mile-long southbound reach.

The Charles bends to the left at a point called Captain's Island that was originally a mound of high ground in the midst of salt marsh. In 1817 the Commonwealth purchased Captain's Island and built a powder magazine there. The ruins of the powder house were rebuilt into a bathhouse, still standing, and Magazine Street retains its name. Acres of the former marsh are now softball fields that are only a

foot above the water in the Basin. Access 52 is near the
swimming pool at Magazine Beach on Captain's Island. The
Metropolitan District Commission built this pool to
accommodate swimmers who had formerly splashed in the
briny Charles at the Captain's Island Bathing Beach.

The right bank was once within Brookline, but a narrow
strip along the river was ceded to Boston. At the Boston
University Bridge (mile 75.3), the town of Brookline is only
a block from the right bank. The Cottage Farm toll bridge
was built here in 1850.

Beyond the Boston University Bridge the Basin opens to
its full width of one-half mile. The buildings of Boston
University are across Storrow Drive on the right bank.
Above and beyond them is the Citgo sign at Kenmore
Square. From the river the Back Bay can be seen standing
on its plain of fill, with the remains of Beacon Hill rising in
the background.

A search for the mouth of Muddy River will reveal a
space of about two inches between the bottom of Storrow
Drive and the surface of the Basin. This represents the top
of the culvert through which Muddy River enters the Basin,
after its sluggish journey through the Fens. In 1866, the
right bank of the Basin was next to Beacon Street from
Muddy River nearly to Charles Street.

Massachusetts Avenue crosses the Charles near the widest point of the Basin, on a bridge four-tenths of a mile long. Twenty-two stone piers support the steel I-beams of the Harvard Bridge, which bustles with joggers and bicycles and autos. When the Harvard Bridge was completed in 1891, Massachusetts Avenue reached Cambridge over a long causeway over mud flats. The flats were filled by a developer and acquired by the Massachusetts Institute of Technology. M.I.T.'s main building was completed in 1916.

Because the wind and the boat traffic can be fierce on this reach of the basin, canoeists sometimes seek the shelter of a series of lagoons that line the right bank. Beacon Street and the townhouses of the Back Bay are a block behind Storrow Drive. Just above the entrance to the first of the lagoons is a concrete boat dock used in nice weather by riverfront loungers. Storrow Lagoon is the most upstream of the chain, reached by passing through a narrow channel and under a footbridge.

Suggested Outings

Canoe
— Explore the Basin in either direction from Captain's Island.
Distance: Variable
Portages: None
Parking: Access 52

Walks
— The universities and parks along the Basin offer first-rate urban walking.

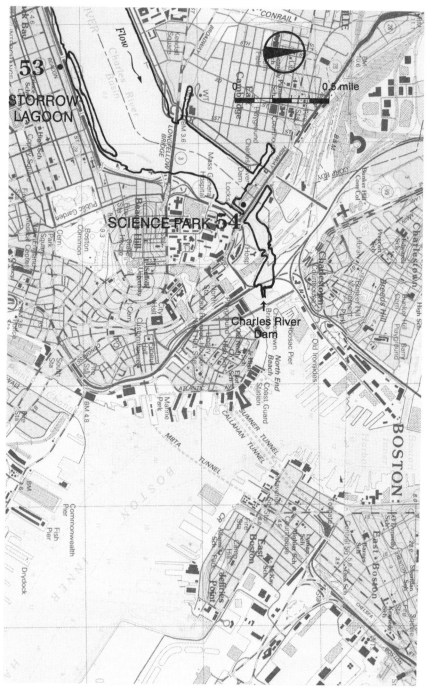

USGS 7.5' × 15': *Boston South*

Charles River: City of Cambridge; Charlestown (City of Boston)

Lower Basin

Access Points

Canoe

53 STORROW LAGOON, Boston (mile 76.6)
USGS Boston South quadrangle
Though most canoe landings must have convenient
automobile parking to qualify as access points, allowances
must be made for downtown Boston. The Esplanade has
easy launching in its sheltered lagoons.

54 SCIENCE PARK (mile 77.7)
USGS Boston South quadrangle
Boston's Museum of Science stands atop the old (1910)
Charles River Dam, with the Basin at its rear. The
museum has a parking garage.

Foot

Boston's Esplanade is reached from the MBTA's Red Line
at the Charles Street Station, or from the Green Line at the
Science Park Station.

Comments

On calm days with light boat traffic, paddlers can enjoy the
full breadth of the Charles River Basin, finding quietness
within the eye of the urban storm that swirls around them.
Here is a unique perspective on the Boston skyline. In other
circumstances canoeists will appreciate the protection of the
sheltered water along the Boston bank, and will choose to
travel in the chain of lagoons. The first or westernmost is
called "Storrow Lagoon." The next is called the
"Canoeway," and the last, near the Hatch Shell, is the "Concert Lagoon."

Alongside the Canoeway, the Esplanade Refreshment

Pavilion offers sustenance to hungry travellers wishing to fortify themselves before braving the lock at the Charles River Dam.

Paddlers emerge from the Concert Lagoon into an area called the "Boat Haven," which has breakwaters to quell waves pushed across the Basin by a west wind. Canoeists continuing downstream are exposed to the swells only briefly before they pass under Longfellow Bridge (mile 77.3), which carries the MBTA Red Line as well as automobile traffic. Beyond Longfellow Bridge is the final section of the Basin. Cambridge Parkway runs along the left bank, ending at the Lechmere Canal just above Science Park. On the right bank Massachusetts General Hospital rises behind a broad segment of the Esplanade.

The old Charles River Dam, now leased to the Museum of Science and dubbed Science Park, is at mile 77.7. This dam was built from 1903 to 1910 to create a scenic water park, and, by halting the ebb and flow of tides, to eliminate the noxious reek of sewage-laden mudflats at low tide. Boats pass through the dam in the lock near the right bank. The MBTA Green Line and the O'Brien Highway pass overhead.

The area below the old dam is likely to be altered in the coming years during improvements to the highway system. In 1991, canoeists encounter the following. At mile 77.9 a railroad drawbridge connects the rail yards of East Cambridge with Boston's North Station. MBTA commuter trains cross this bridge en route to terminals at Gardner, Lowell, Haverhill, Ipswich, and Rockport. There is enough headroom under the bridge for canoeists when the draw is closed. The immense I-beams are painted the color of copper.

The Fitzgerald Expressway is high above the Charles at mile 78.1, carrying the traffic of Route 93 and Route 1. The expressway overlooks the new Charles River Dam, which has three locks for moving boats between the Basin and the harbor. Two locks are 200 feet long and 25 feet wide, and the third is 300 feet long and 40 feet wide. A green light indicates when to enter a lock. To get the attention of the person who controls the lock, four blasts of a whistle or air-horn might be necessary — the official signal is two long, two short. Signs instruct boaters to grasp ropes which are attached to floats along the side of the lock and rise and fall with the water.

When the gates at the lower end of the lock are opened, the canoeist is released into tidal waters at the mouth of the Charles. Boston Harbor, Massachusetts Bay, and the Atlantic Ocean are at hand; no further works of humanity impede navigation, and adventurous canoeists occasionally strike out for destinations across the harbor, such as the mouth of the Neponset River. By canoeing up the Neponset to Mother Brook, Boston can be circumnavigated. It is hazardous to canoe in ocean water because, in the event of an accident, cold water rapidly depletes the energies of a person in the water. Most canoeists will be content with having reached salt water, and will take out on the harbor side of the dam near the Metropolitan District Commission Police Station or will return to the Basin through the lock.

Suggested Outings

Canoe
— Visit the Esplanade's lagoons.
Parking: Access 52.

Walks
— The south and east shores of the Charles River Basin present Boston walkers with a broad expanse of light and air. Reach the Esplanade. Access 53, by the way of the MBTA's Red or Green Lines.

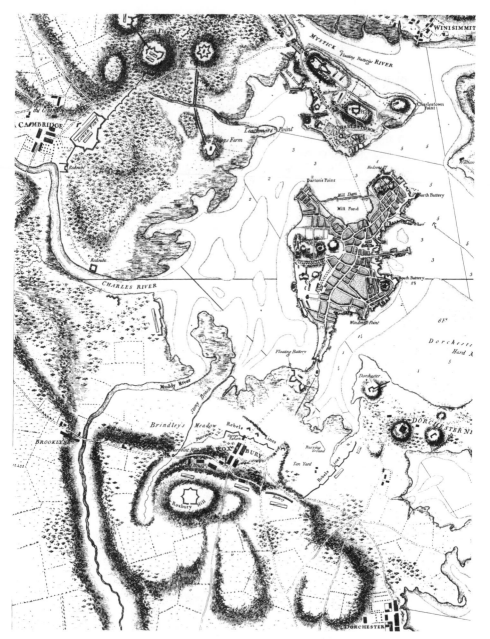

Charles River Estuary, 1775

Detail from map drawn by a British soldier during the occupation of Boston.
BOSTON, MASSACHUSETTS AND VICINITY IN 1775.
Reproduced from an engraving in the Cornell University Library.

Charles River Basin Study Area

Before the Charles River Dam closed out the sea in 1908, the river's estuary began at Watertown. In estuaries, fresh water mixes with salt, tides come and go twice each day, and a specialized community of plants and animals takes advantage of the unique environment. The broad salt marshes along the lower Charles provided warm-water nurseries for infant sea creatures as well as feeding and nesting habitat for shore birds. Former marshes are now occupied by the campus of the Harvard Business School and by the Victorian town houses of Boston's Back Bay.

As the salt marshes were filled, the cleansing effect of their vegetation was lost. The urban population mushroomed in the late 1800s, and so did the problems of waste disposal. At low tide the mudflats along the Charles reeked of sewage. It was proposed in 1894 by the Metropolitan Park Commission and the State Board of Health that the tides be excluded from the lower Charles by the construction of a dam. But the practicality and expense of the creation of a Basin required years of examination and vigorous debate. There was concern that the "fresh water" would actually be a large pool of odiferous, stagnant sewage. Engineers eventually concluded that this fate could be avoided, and proponents of the dam carried the day. The dam was built where the Craigie Bridge had stood. In 1908 the tides were excluded and the Basin began to fill, and in 1910 the project was completed.

The dam did not adequately protect Boston from flooding, and the hurricanes of the 1950s caused extensive damage. At one point, the Basin rose four and one-half feet above its normal level. A new dam was designed with the ability to pump water out of the Basin into the harbor, but no funds were available to build it until, in the mid-1960s, the Army Corps of Engineers entered the picture. Congress authorized the New England Division of the Corps to study the situation and make recommendations. This resulted in the Natural Valley Storage Project (see page 24) and in the construction of the new dam from 1974 to 1978. The Corps built the dam and turned it over to the Metropolitan District Commission, which began regular operations of the dam in 1981. At that time the locks and sluices of the 1910 dam were permanently opened.

The six pumps in the Charles River Dam are capable of discharging a total of 8,400 cubic feet per second against a nine-foot head. The largest flow in the Charles since 1876, as measured at Waltham's Moody Street Dam, was 4,150 cubic feet per second, recorded on February 3, 1976, when an ice dam gave way, releasing water it had detained upstream. Although this figure is comfortably under the capacity of the dam's pumps, they must be able to remove runoff entering the Basin in addition to the flow measured by the gauge at Waltham.

The Esplanade evolved. Park development began around 1890 with a playground designed by the landscape architect Frederick Law Olmsted. During the construction of the 1910 dam a seawall was built along the Boston side of the river, backfilled with material dredged from the riverbed. Officially named the Boston Embankment, it became known as the Esplanade. The last stages of what is now Boston's riverfront were designed by Arthur A. Shurcliff, a landscape architect who had trained under one of Olmsted's partners, Charles Eliot. The Hatch Shell was built in 1939. The Esplanade was named the Storrow Memorial Embankment because Helen Storrow, the widow of James J. Storrow, gave a million dollars to help pay for Basin improvements. Storrow Drive was built in the early 1950s, and the chain of lagoons, boat landings, and footbridges were completed in this period, when Shurcliff designed an expanded embankment to accommodate the new highway.

Part Two:
History

Native Americans

People have lived along the Charles River for at least 9000 years. During the period between 3000 and 5000 years ago, New England's population of hunters-gatherers left more artifacts along the Charles than did those who preceded or followed them, which suggests that the inland population was highest at this time. These people, called "Archaic" by archaeologists, occupied sites along the Charles and other Massachusetts rivers. They depended on the productive community of plants and animals found in the river valleys. In the estuary of the Charles, Archaic people built a large weir, which is called the Boylston Street Fish Weir. This was a fence of basketry supported by posts, which trapped fish as the tide went out.

By the time the Europeans arrived, the upper and middle portions of the Charles River Basin were thinly populated. The natives had come to depend on agriculture. Because of the longer growing season and the availability of seafood, most of the population lived near the seacoast. Indian farmers grew corn, beans, tobacco, and squash including pumpkins and zucchini. During the fall and winter, groups moved farther inland to hunt deer, bear, beaver, raccoon, rabbit, and muskrat, and to gather berries, nuts, seeds, and roots.

All of the natives from the Maritime Provinces to North Carolina spoke languages of the Eastern Algonquian family. Massachusetts Algonquian was spoken from the Saco River to Cape Cod, but not all of its speakers belonged to the Massachusetts tribe, which was a group of sachemdoms around Boston Harbor — the coastal indentation that receives the waters of the Mystic, Charles, and Neponset Rivers. Dialects of Massachusetts Algonquian were spoken by Nipmucks who lived to the west, Penacook (also called Pawtucket) to the north, and by Wampanoags to the south.

Exploration and Founding
of the Massachusetts Colonies

When Giovanni da Verrazano sailed into Narragansett Bay
in 1524 he was welcomed by a score of dugout canoes containing friendly natives who traded furs for glass jewelry. In
the years following, European ships came to New England
seeking codfish, and Massachusetts Bay was visited
repeatedly. By the end of the 1500s the New England coast
had been explored and mapped. New England's fish, fur,
and timber were of value to Europeans, though of course
the absence of precious metals was disappointing.

In 1602 a group of English merchants sent Bartholomew
Gosnold to investigate the potential profitability of New
World commodities. He fished off Provincetown and gave
names to Cape Cod, Martha's Vineyard, and the Elizabeth
Islands. He carried home a profitable cargo of sassafras and
enthusiasm about the commercial potential of New England.
As a result of Gosnold's voyage, the following spring
another group of businessmen sent Martin Pring to harvest
two shiploads of sassafras, which was sweet and flavorful,
and thought to be of medicinal value. Pring spent seven
weeks at the future site of Plymouth while his ships were
loaded with fragrant cargo. His reports of the bountiful
crops of the native farmers encouraged the belief that
Massachusetts could support a colony.

An English sponsor of these voyages, Sir Ferdinando
Gorges, formed an enduring interest in settlement of New
England. In 1607 he attempted to found a community at the
mouth of the Kennebec River called Sagadahoc Colony. A
severe winter, a fire in the storehouse, and violent conflicts
with the Indians prompted the survivors to return to
England in 1608.

Meanwhile, the French were active. In 1605 they
established Port Royal at present-day Annapolis, Nova
Scotia. From this base Samuel de Champlain explored the
New England coast as far south as Woods Hole. His written
account of these expeditions is one of the principal
documents describing New England before colonization.
Champlain is credited with the European discovery of Boston Harbor and therefore of the Charles River. He called
the harbor the Baye des Isles. But the French saw no
advantage here to tempt them away from Nova Scotia, so
Massachusetts Bay had no white settlers when John Smith
arrived in 1614.

Smith, employed as an explorer by the Northern Virginia Company, made the best map to date of the coast from Penobscot Bay to Cape Cod. His map gave Plymouth, Cape Ann, and the Charles River their English names. Smith originally referred to the river after the people who lived along it: the Massachusetts. Back in England Smith either flattered his prince by naming the Massachusetts' river after him, or stood by as Prince Charles named it for himself. In 1625 the prince became King Charles I, whose oppressions motivated the Puritan exodus to America.

There is a mistaken tradition that the Algonquians called the river Quinobequin. This resulted from an error on the part of an eighteenth century mapmaker who confused the Charles with the Kennebec, which Smith spelled "Quinobequin." Phonetic interpretations of Algonquian place names varied widely.

Sassafras was one of Massachusetts' earliest exports.

163

Smith was impressed with "the Countrie of the Massachusetts," and he compared it favorably to the less hospitable climate and soil of Maine, which he had visited in the spring. He wrote of Massachusetts, "Could I have but the meanes to transport a Colonie, I would rather live here than anywhere." Misled by the broad estuary of the Charles, Smith surmised that "the River doth pearce many daies journies the intralles of that Countrey."

While Smith had commanded one of the ships on the Northern Virginia Company's expedition of 1614, a second vessel was under Thomas Hunt. After a period of fishing off the coast of Maine, Hunt sailed to Plymouth and kidnapped twenty native men. He picked up seven more at Cape Cod, carried them to Spain, and sold them for twenty pounds apiece. This act was condemned by John Smith and others, and was infamous among the Indians. One of those enslaved was named Squanto.

Squanto somehow migrated from Spain to England and eventually to Newfoundland, where in 1618 he met Thomas Dermer, who was on his way to trade in Massachusetts. Dermer recognized the potential value of Squanto as a guide and translator and took him along. Dermer found that a drastic change had come to Plymouth and to Massachusetts Bay. Most of the people were gone. Squanto's Patuxet Wampanoags, formerly a village of 200, had been wiped out by an infectious disease to which the Indians had no resistance. All of the coastal tribes had terrible losses. No one knows what the sickness was. Smallpox, plague, chicken pox, measles, and scarlet fever are all listed as possibilities; it is taken for granted that the disease was of European origin. Puritan settlers thought that Divine Providence had rid Massachusetts Bay of the biggest obstacle to settlement and left cleared fields for their convenience. It is estimated that for the area between Saco Bay in Maine and Narragansett Bay in Rhode Island, the population of native coastal peoples was reduced from 100,000 in 1617 to 5,000 by 1619.

Dermer liberated Squanto, which was a successful conciliatory gesture to Massasoit, the Wampanoag sachem. In a diplomatic sense, this paved the way for the Pilgrims, who came to Plymouth in December of 1620. Of the 102 passengers on the *Mayflower,* 41 were Separatists, and only 27 of these were adults. The Separatists journeyed to the New World to practice their

Protestant orthodoxy in safety. The other 61 Pilgrims
came to Plymouth for secular reasons. Although the
strong-willed Separatists dominated the colony's politics,
Plymouth lacked the feverish self-righteousness that
characterized the Massachusetts Bay Colony in the 1600s.

The winter diet of the Pilgrims was inadequate, and
their hastily constructed buildings did not offer good
shelter. Only fifty survived until the spring of 1621, when
the Wampanoags came to call. The Pilgrims greeted
Massasoit with suitable pomp, established the peace, and
obtained the assistance of Squanto. Before his death eighteen months later, Squanto had taught the English the
practical skills they needed to survive and had served as
interpreter during the all-important treaty negotiations
with Massasoit.

It was news of the scarcity of the natives and of the
Pilgrim's peaceful coexistence with the surviving Wampanoags that led, a few years later, to the massive migration of Puritans to Massachusetts Bay. Meanwhile, there
was an influx of adventurers to Plymouth. Some of these
stayed within the colony but others spread out, taking up
land around the bay. One was a man named William
Blackstone (also spelled Blaxton) who established himself
on the side of a hill on a peninsula at the mouth of the
Charles River. He was the first resident of Beacon Hill.
From his arrival in about 1624, Blackstone farmed, traded
for furs, and studied his books until the Puritans came at
the end of the decade.

By 1628, political and economic developments in
England had caused a union of interests between Puritan
leaders and a group of middle-class businessmen. They
decided to seek their futures in New England. The
Massachusetts Bay Company, chartered in August of 1629
at Cambridge, England, was granted all of the land from
three miles south of the Charles River to three miles
north of the Merrimack River, and west to the "South
Sea," as the Pacific Ocean was then named. A tiny colony
had been established at Salem in 1626. It was much
expanded by new arrivals sent by the Massachusetts Bay
Company. By the summer of 1629 so many English had
disembarked at Salem that some were diverted to a new
outpost at Charlestown. John Winthrop, governor of the
colony, reached Charlestown on the ship *Arbella* in June
of 1630. He brought with him the charter of the
Massachusetts Bay Company, thus showing that the

colony's seat of power was to be in America, not in England.

Winthrop, his deputy, and eighteen "assistants" formed the government of the Massachusetts Bay Colony. Their first meeting was in Charlestown on August 23, 1630. In 1632, the colony's freemen (churchmember-voters) were included in a "General Court," which had broad powers. After 1634, the freemen elected representatives to the General Court.

The encampment at Charlestown grew to 800 settlers. Because they lacked water and suffered from disease, they were compelled to disperse. By the end of September, 1630, six new towns had begun: Watertown, Roxbury, Dorchester, Medford, Saugus, and, on the Shawmut Peninsula, Boston. Already the population of Massachusetts Bay Colony had eclipsed that of the "Old Colony" at Plymouth. The two colonies were legally united in 1690.

The decade between 1630 and 1640 is known as the Great Migration, which brought twenty thousand immigrants to New England. Immigration slowed drastically in 1641 because Puritans had taken over the government of England, and their need for escape disappeared. But by that time colonists were well established in the valley of the Charles.

Charles River Towns

A river is superior to a lake in its liberating influence.
It has motion and indefinite length. A river touching
the back of a town is like a wing. River towns are
winged towns.

Henry David Thoreau
from his journal, July 2, 1858

When first settled by English colonists, land in the
watershed of the Charles River was assigned by the
General Court to a few large towns. In the course of time
these towns divided into smaller entities. Because their
histories are closely related, communities are grouped
according to their parentage.

Boston and Brookline

Boston

William Blackstone's old friend Isaac Johnson arrived in
Charlestown in the summer of 1630. Blackstone invited
Johnson and Governor Winthrop to join him on the Shawmut Peninsula, where springs provided plenty of fresh
water. At first Shawmut had seemed too small to the
Puritans. It did not have much farmland, and, because it
had little timber, wood had to be hauled from harbor
islands. Worst of all, Shawmut was vulnerable to attack
from the sea. But the water supply was good, the location
was central to the bay, and there was a good harbor on
the east side of the peninsula. William Wood, an early
visitor, observed, "It being a Necke and bare of wood,
they are not troubled with three great annoyances of
Woolves, Rattlesnakes, and Musketoes." Furthermore, the
narrow neck could be easily fortified against the Indians.

Fear of Indians overcame fear of the seafaring French.
Though they had intended to manage the colony from
Newtowne (Cambridge), the Puritans in 1632 made Boston their capital. The General Court voted that William
Blackstone was to have fifty acres set out for him. Two
years later, Boston bought this land from Blackstone, pay-
ing thirty pounds for its new Common. Blackstone was
moving on. He supposedly told his new neighbors "I came
from England because I did not like the Lord Bishops, but
I can not join with you because I would not be under the
Lords Brethren." He purchased some cattle and moved to
the river that became the Blackstone, where he built a
house called Study Hall in present-day Cumberland,

Rhode Island. In 1659 Blackstone married a widow. He died at the age of seventy-six in 1675. His papers were destroyed during King Philip's War.

Because the Shawmut Peninsula was dominated by a hill with three summits, the town was at first called Trimountain. In September of 1630 it was named Boston after a town in England, home of some of the settlers. Tremont Street reflects the original name. In 1635, a beacon was erected on the highest of the hills to warn of danger. The beacon was a barrel of pitch set atop a pole. The pitch was to have been ignited in the event of enemy attack. The light would have been visible in most of the colony's settlements. It was never used, but the name of Beacon Hill has endured.

Boston's first houses were built near boat landings on the east side of the peninsula. The town spread from this center, which is the present location of the Old State House and Dock Square. Boston of the 1600s communicated with the world primarily through boats, and secondarily by the road through the narrow neck to Roxbury. The town grew to cover the land that nature had provided Shawmut, then added to its acreage by filling along the shorelines. In the 1800s, most of Trimountain was spread around Shawmut Peninsula's periphery to expand its land area. Trimountain was of glacial origin; since it did not have a core of bedrock, it was easily removed. The first peak to go was the westernmost hill, called Mount Vernon and sometimes Mount Whoredom in recognition of the non-puritanical neighborhood on its north side. Material that had formed the summit of Mt. Vernon was removed in 1799 and transported by gravity railroad to the western edge of the Common, which was at that time the riverbank, to create Charles Street and the Public Garden.

When the new State House was built on Beacon Hill in 1795, the summit of the hill rose behind it, surmounted with a memorial to the events that led to the American Revolution. The hill belonged to John Hancock, who had provided land for the new State House. His heirs inherited most of the top of Beacon Hill, and in 1810 they sold it. For the next dozen years its substance was conveyed by tip cart to the Mill Pond in the cove at the north end of the peninsula.

The eastern peak was called Pemberton or Cotton Hill. It was reduced in 1835 and used to further extend the North End.

Through all this time the Back Bay was still wetland. It was far too large to be filled by Shawmut's hills. Instead, a dam was built across its mouth. When completed in 1821 the dam was a mile and a half long and fifty feet wide. The toll road on its top became an extension of Beacon Street. The enclosure was divided by a cross dam, so that two mill ponds were created; one to store water at high tide, and another to receive water after it had turned the mill wheels.

The tracks of the Boston and Worcester Railroad crossed these big ponds on trestles. In the railroad was power great enough to fill the Back Bay, and in 1858 the task was begun. Gravel was brought from Needham by way of the Charles River Branch Railroad. With breathtaking efficiency, sand, stone, and gravel were loaded into cars by steamshovels built at the Globe Locomotive Works in South Boston. A pair of steamshovels could load a train in ten minutes. Trains of thirty-five cars each ran night and day, one round trip every forty-five minutes during the day, and only a little less often during the night. When this process began, dry land ended at the western end of the Public Garden. By 1861, Arlington, Berkeley, and Clarendon Streets were in place, and by 1882 the Back Bay was filled. The resulting profile of Boston is visible from a boat in the Basin, from which the remains of Beacon Hill can be discerned as well as the unnaturally level topography of the Back Bay.

Brookline

In the early years of New England, livestock was allowed to forage freely. Cultivated crops had to be fenced to protect them from marauding cows and pigs. Boston's pioneer farmers hit upon an easier strategy: move the livestock off the peninsula during the crop-growing months. Though the land just across Boston Neck belonged to the town of Roxbury, there was unused land along the Charles River, across the saltmarsh of the Back Bay. The area took its name from the stream that drained it, Muddy River. Boston claimed this land for itself, and used it as a cow pasture and as a source of wood.

Allotments of land began in 1635. John Cotton, Boston's minister, was given a farm of 250 acres, but the Cotton family did not live there. As the years went by a few families left the security of Boston to take up residence at Muddy River Hamlet. By 1660 about twenty-five households made up the village. At the turn of the century there were enough families to justify Muddy River's separation from Boston. In 1705 Brookline was incorporated as a separate town, bounded on the north by the Charles River, on the east by the Back Bay and Roxbury, on the south by Dedham, and on the west by Newton.

Brookline had been the name of a farm on the west side of town, on Smelt Brook, owned by a prominent citizen named Judge Sewall. At the time of incorporation, Brookline was adopted as a name for the town. As the area urbanized, Smelt Brook disappeared.

For its first century Brookline was an agricultural town, producing food for its increasingly urban parent community. After 1800, farmers began to sell their land to well-to-do Bostonians, who established country estates. The construction of the Boston and Worcester Railroad in 1833 bisected Brookline and destined the town to become a residential suburb. In 1855 Brookline ceded to Boston a narrow strip of land along the Charles River. Boston attempted to annex the rest of Brookline in the 1870s, but Brookline marshalled enough political clout to resist the loss of its independence.

Cambridge, Newton, and West Roxbury

Cambridge

Cambridge was settled in 1631. It was originally called Newtowne, and was envisioned as the capital of the Massachusetts Bay Colony. Watertown and Charlestown, which lay west and east of Newtowne, were considered exposed to Indian attack; it was felt that Newtowne should be fortified. A palisade was constructed in the area that is now Harvard Square.

Newtowne's pioneers were disappointed in their expectation that their town would be the political center of the colony, because Governor Winthrop changed his mind and set up his residence in Boston. The colony's government consoled Newtowne by awarding it another distinction. In 1636 the General Court appropriated 400 pounds to establish a college. It was decided that the school should be at Newtowne, and that the town's name should be changed to Cambridge, after the English university that had trained the most important Puritan leaders. There was not enough money to establish the school until the following year, when John Harvard bequeathed the college 700 pounds and his library. The General Court named the school after its benefactor.

Bounded by Watertown and Charlestown, Cambridge felt hemmed in and short of land. In 1638 Boston offered lands to the south of the Charles River. For the next fifty years, Cambridge straddled the Charles. Newton was set off as a separate town in 1688. In 1713, Lexington was set off. In 1807, the last part of Cambridge to the south of the Charles became Brighton, which was annexed to the city of Boston in 1874.

Harvard, the intellectual center of the entire colony, was the central feature of the Cambridge economy until the arrival of railroads and industry in the mid-1800s. At one time or another, Cambridge has supported a variety of large-scale industries: printing, baking, the production of candy and ice cream, meat packing, and the manufacture of musical and optical instruments, pumps, electrical machinery, fishing nets, furniture, soap, and sheet metal.

In 1916 the Massachusetts Institute of Technology moved from Boston to a new campus built at the Cambridge end of the Harvard Bridge.

Newton
One of the objectives in the king's charter of the Massachusetts Bay Company was the conversion of the Indians to Christianity. Roxbury's minister, John Eliot, began to study the Massachusetts Algonquian language in 1641, with the objective of preaching to the Indians in their own tongue. His study lasted five years. In October of 1646 Eliot rode to Nonantum, a stockaded Indian village on the south side of the Charles not far from the Watertown mill. The people of Nonantum were a sub-tribe of the Massachusetts led by a sachem named Waban. Eliot's first sermon lasted more than an hour. His text was Ezekiel 37:9, "Then said he unto me, prophesy unto the wind," which caused the Indians to look at each other, and Waban to smile. The Algonquian word for wind was Waban.

Charles River
Towns and Cities

Parent towns are shown in bold type; towns
which appear to their right were set off from
them or incorporated on the dates indicated.

† These towns were annexed to Boston:
Charlestown in 1873; Brighton, Roxbury and
West Roxbury in 1874.

* Medway and Millis are on land granted to
Medfield and were never part of Dedham.

Map at right indicates town and city locations
along the Charles River, with their dates of
incorporation.

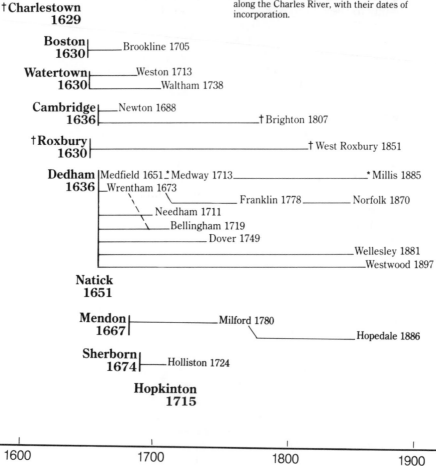

† Charlestown
1629

Boston
1630 —— Brookline 1705

Watertown —————Weston 1713
1630 ————————Waltham 1738

Cambridge —— Newton 1688
1636 ————————————————† Brighton 1807

† Roxbury
1630 ——————————————————————————† West Roxbury 1851

Dedham Medfield 1651 * Medway 1713————————————————* Millis 1885
1636 Wrentham 1673
                       ————————— Franklin 1778————————— Norfolk 1870
                  ——— Needham 1711
                  ———Bellingham 1719
                       ————— Dover 1749
                                                              ————Wellesley 1881
                                                              ————Westwood 1897

Natick
1651

Mendon ———————— Milford 1780
1667
                              ———————————— Hopedale 1886

Sherborn
1674 ——— Holliston 1724

Hopkinton
1715

1600	1700	1800	1900

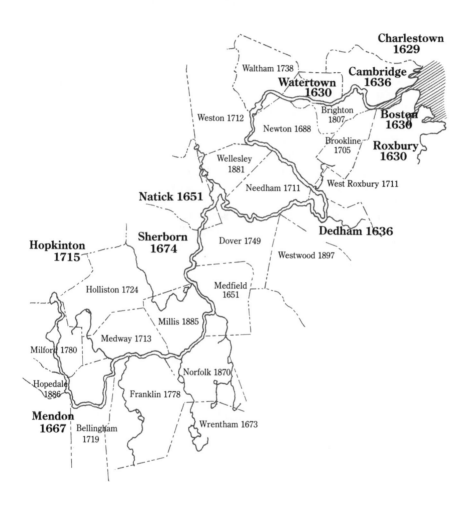

Charlestown
1629

Cambridge
1636

Waltham 1738

Watertown
1630

Weston 1712

Brighton
1807

Boston
1630

Newton 1688

Brookline
1705

Roxbury
1630

Wellesley
1881

West Roxbury 1711

Needham 1711

Natick 1651

Dedham 1636

Hopkinton
1715

Sherborn
1674

Dover 1749

Westwood 1897

Holliston 1724

Medfield
1651

Millis 1885

Milford 1780

Medway 1713

Hopedale
1886

Norfolk 1870

Mendon
1667

Franklin 1778

Bellingham
1719

Wrentham 1673

Waban's people were surrounded by potential enemies. They were exposed to the Nipmucks to the west, to the Wampanoags and Narragansetts to the south, and to the English to the north and east. Waban apparently felt it wise to ally his people with the English, and in John Eliot he found a sympathetic and effective liaison. He immediately requested that his people be "granted" the land on which they lived. Eliot proposed this to the General Court, and it was done. Eliot returned to Nonantum every other week throughout the winter, and, as it turned out, continued preaching to Waban's people for the rest of his life.

It was soon evident that Nonantum was too near the English towns. Some of the whites were willing to exploit their Indian neighbors. At Eliot's suggestion the General Court in 1648 prohibited the selling of spirits to Indians. A search for a suitable site for an Indian town was begun. Eventually Natick was settled on and was obtained from Dedham, and Waban and his people moved there in 1651. Their story is continued on page 183.

By the time the "praying Indians" left, white settlers were well established in Newton. Of the eleven villages that form the city, the first to be settled was Newton Corner, where the Fuller farm was purchased in 1638. Newton's first grist mill was powered by Hyde Brook. Eventually there were enough farms to the south of the river to justify the creation of a new town. "Cambridge Village" was set off from the rest of Cambridge in 1688, and named Newtown three years later. In 1766, Judge Abraham Fuller altered the spelling to Newton.

Although Newton eventually became a bedroom community, for a long time it was an industrial and agricultural town. The industries clustered at the falls in the Charles River. Industrial development at Upper Falls is described on page 124, Lower Falls on page 182, and Bemis on page 139.

After the Boston and Worcester Railroad opened, Newton began to become a residential suburb. The railroad reached Newton Corner on April 16, 1833. The following year it pushed west through Newtonville, West Newton, Auburndale, and across the Charles at Riverside to "Grantville," the future Wellesley Hills. Newton was on its way to becoming "The Garden City."

West Roxbury

Joseph Weld, one of Roxbury's early settlers, took up land on the west end of the town in 1643. He received his estate from the Massachusetts Bay Colony as a reward for his success in making a treaty with the Pequod Indians. The area was called Jamaica End. By 1706 there were forty-five families living west of Jamaica Pond. They began to press for separation, which was granted in 1711.

In 1838 West Roxbury received some land along the Charles that had been the southern tip of Newton. In 1840 George and Sophia Ripley spent a summer on a dairy farm in this part of town. Ripley was a Unitarian minister who had concluded that if humans took action to improve this world, the hereafter would take care of itself. In pursuit of their ideals, Ripley and like-minded associates bought the farm. In a letter to Ralph Waldo Emerson, Ripley explained that the purpose of Brook Farm was:

> to insure a more natural union between intellectual and manual labor than now exists; to combine the thinker and the worker, as far as possible, in the same individual; to guarantee the highest mental freedom, by providing all with labor adapted to their tastes and talents, and securing to them the fruits of their industry; to do away with the necessity of menial services by opening the benefits of education and the profits of labor to all; and thus to prepare a society of liberal, intelligent, and cultivated persons, whose relationships with each other would permit a more wholesome and simple life than can be led amidst the pressure of our competitive institutions.

In April of 1841 the Ripleys and a dozen others, including Nathaniel Hawthorne, moved into Brook Farm. Several of the principals, including George Ripley, were associated with the group of philosophers called Transcendentalists. Transcendentalists who did not move to Brook Farm were nonetheless very much aware of it. Thoreau's solitary stay at Walden Pond, for example, began during the Brook Farm years and was in conscious contrast with the farm's endeavor in group living.

From 1841 until 1846, Brook Farm flourished, at least in its importance to those who spent some of their lives there. Though neither Brook Farm nor a similar idealistic experiment upriver in Hopedale succeeded as enduring economic enterprises, their participants made themselves heard as defenders of the freedom and dignity of individual humans. These communities were part of a reform movement that helped America's agrarian democratic political institutions survive the industrial revolution.

The last of Brook Farm's buildings burned in 1985. The sites of the farm buildings are reached from the entrance road to Gethsemane Cemetery (see page 110).

West Roxbury was annexed to Boston in January, 1874.

Watertown, Weston, and Waltham

Watertown

When the English first visited Watertown in May of 1630, 300 Indians were camped there. The place was called Pequog, and the people the Pequossette, a subtribe of the Massachusetts. They grew crops near the river, and fished at the falls. The Pequosette offered their guests a large fish, which was gladly accepted. This group of English eventually settled at Dorchester.

In July of the same year, a group led by Richard Saltonstall arrived intending to stay. Saltonstall was one of the eighteen members of the colony's Court of Assistants, and had helped the Massachusetts Bay Company obtain its charter. He, his minister, and the people of the parish landed near the location of the Eliot Bridge. In the years to follow, the center of the town shifted upriver toward the rapids.

Watertown was the first of the Bay Colony's inland towns. Because the colonial charter extended indefinitely westward, Watertown originally stretched to the Pacific Ocean. The settlers found an attractive park-like landscape, the result of the Indians having burned off underbrush. The soil was fertile, and there were springs of fresh water. The Pequosette showed the settlers how to build wigwams in which to live while they built houses.

The minister of the Watertown pioneers was George Phillips, whose descendants founded the Phillips Academies of Andover and Exeter. Another of his descendants was the first mayor of Boston. George Phillips was a theological liberal; in contrast with some of the Puritan leaders, he respected the opinions of others. Though Richard Saltonstall had political troubles and returned to England in 1631, Phillips remained an important figure in Watertown for many years.

The rapids at Watertown marked the uppermost reach of the ocean tides. At spawning time herring and shad came upstream in huge numbers. The town built a weir in which more than 100,000 fish were taken on some spring days! Fish were used for fertilizer, or were preserved by drying or salting, and shipped to England in barrels.

The first mill on the Charles was built at the falls by Thomas Mayhew in 1634. It ground wheat, rye, and corn. A fulling mill was added in 1686, and subsequently there were saw, paper, chocolate, and cotton mills. In 1855 a foundry was built that made cannon balls for the Civil War. Water power went out of use about 1900. In 1966 a new dam was built, and a fish ladder was added in 1972.

The area at the Watertown rapids had long been a place to cross the Charles. It was used as a ford by the Massachusetts, who had villages on both sides of the river there. Even today the water below the dam is shallow. The first footbridge was built near the mill in 1647. Twenty years later a new bridge was constructed, strong enough to support both human beings and horses. In 1719 a horse-cart bridge was built.

In 1636, when some of its townspeople headed upriver for Dedham. Watertown was the most populous town in the Bay Colony, and was divided into three districts: eastern, middle and western. The western district became Weston, the middle district was eventually divided between Waltham and Belmont, and the eastern district remains as the Watertown of today.

Weston and Waltham
In the early days Watertowners called the part of their town that became Weston "the farms" and "West Pine Meadows." There was a grist mill on Stony Brook as early as 1679, and a cotton mill by 1831. Weston was set off as a separate town in 1712. Part of Weston was included in the new town of Lincoln in 1754. In the mid-1800s, Weston farmers began selling their land to affluent Bostonians, who set up estates in the town. Like Brookline and Newton, Weston became an early suburban residential town because the Boston and Worcester Railroad made commuting possible.

Though Waltham was explored as early as 1632, it was settled slowly and had a population of only 500 when it was incorporated in 1738. At that time it had no streets and no village center. It did have the busiest road to New York, then called the Sudbury Highway, now Route 20. Numerous Waltham taverns served travellers.

In 1788 water power at Waltham's fall on the Charles River was harnessed for the making of paper, but it was cotton that made Waltham famous as a pioneer industrial city, at the initiative of Francis Cabot Lowell and his associates. Lowell was born in Newburyport in 1775, and graduated from Harvard in 1793. After studying manufacturing methods in England, Lowell decided to try to create a large-scale manufacture of cotton cloth in the United States. He and his partners formed the Boston Manufacturing Company and bought the water privilege at Waltham. They built a five-story building at the fall, which survives as the section of the mill nearest the dam. Lowell hired a skilled and inventive mechanic named Paul Moody, whose name is preserved in one of Waltham's central streets. Moody set up the machinery in the new mill, and production began in 1816. Lowell died the next year, but the Boston Manufacturing Company survived and prospered.

The success of Lowell's enterprise led his company to seek greater water power to expand its operations. This power was found at East Chelmsford, which was transformed into an industrial center, and named for Lowell.

The Boston Manufacturing Company hired mostly young women from farms. The first weavers made $2.75 for working seventy-two hours per week. . .and paid back $1.75 for room and board. A pay cut in 1821 caused a work stoppage at the mill, the first known industrial strike in the country. The Boston Manufacturing Company went out of business in 1929. The mill buildings have been converted to publicly supported housing for the elderly, artists' studios, and commercial uses.

In 1849 Waltham gained territory from Newton on the south side of the river. This land, which had been sparsely settled and not good for farming, quickly became part of Waltham's urban center. In the 1850s, Aaron L. Dennison built the American Waltham Watch Company's factory on the right bank of the Charles. Dennison had seen muskets being made from interchangeable parts at the United States Armory at Springfield. He set out to mass-produce watches by making interchangeable watch components by machine. At first the public resisted this idea, and the company was not successful until the Civil War, when the inexpensive watches became popular with soldiers.

Dedham, Needham, Wellesley, Dover, and Westwood

Dedham

Halfway through the decade of the Puritans' Great Migration and five years after its founding, Watertown was feeling population pressure. Good farmland was becoming scarce. Hay, because it provided winter food for cattle and horses, was as vital then as petroleum is now. Oxen (neutered male cattle) were particularly important as draft animals in this era. Broad, grassy meadows spread alongside portions of the Charles and Concord Rivers. The need for hay drew farmers to Concord and Sudbury in the watershed of the Concord River, and to Dedham on the Charles.

In 1635 the General Court granted some venturesome residents of Watertown permission to move up the Charles River and negotiate with the native landowners. The sachem Chickatabot sold William Pynchon land between the Charles and Neponset Rivers. In March of 1636 bounds were set by the General Court. Because the course of the Charles River was only vaguely understood, Dedham was assigned more land than had been intended. The original grant included land that became the towns of Dedham, Norwood, Walpole, Norfolk, Wrentham, Franklin, Medfield, Needham, Dover, and most of Bellingham. The proprietors proposed that their settlement be named Contentment, along the hopeful lines of Concord and Salem (which was a version of *shalom*, the Hebrew word for peace). But the General Court named the new town Dedham in honor of some new immigrants from that English town. The family names of some of Dedham's founders were Carter, Alleyn, Shaw, Morse, Dalton, Dwight, and Rogers. A few pioneers moved to Dedham in the winter of 1636-1637, but the bulk of the proprietors settled in the spring of 1637.

The new town needed a mill to saw logs into boards and to grind grain, but an attempt to found a mill on the Charles River came to nothing. The town decided that

East Brook, a tributary of the Neponset River, would offer excellent mill sites if it could be provided with more water. In 1639 Dedhamites dug a ditch through Purchase Meadow, diverting Charles River water to the head of East Brook, which became known as Mother Brook. From that day to this, the Charles has fed the Neponset. Local farmers applauded the diversion on the theory that it helped drain water from the hayfields of the river meadows. Eventually, suits were brought by those who ran mills downstream on the Charles and wanted the water. After lengthy litigation, the transfer from one river basin to another was allowed to continue. Today the diversion continues under the supervision of the Metropolitan District Commission, which uses Mother Brook to maintain parity in the flows of the Neponset and the Charles.

By 1649 Dedham's demand for meadow again exceeded its supply. Some farmers had taken hay in the area the Indians called "Bogastow," the broad valley above Sherborn. That part of Bogastow that lay east of the river was within the bounds of Dedham, but it was far from the village. Dedham decided to establish a new town, and to ask the General Court to grant additional land west of the Charles, which it did. The new town was Medfield. The lands granted in 1649 were at first part of Medfield, but became the towns of Medway and Millis.

Dedham was within Suffolk County, one of the original counties of Massachusetts. In 1680, the first Norfolk County was extinguished by the formation of New Hampshire. When it was found desirable to divide Suffolk County, in 1793, the name of Norfolk County was revived, and Dedham was named the county seat. In the course of spawning towns that themselves separated into towns of the second and third generations, the center of Dedham developed a diverse industrial base. It was connected to the metropolis by the main line of the Norfolk County Railroad and supplied with dependable water power tapped from the Charles and released to the Neponset. As a county seat, it gained legal and political importance. Dedham grew into one of the bustling quasi-urban planets within a near orbit of Boston.

Needham
The policy of the Massachusetts Bay Colony required two stages of negotiation before land could be settled. First,

180

permission had to be obtained from the General Court in the form of a grant. Second, the land had to be purchased from its native holders through the highest local authority, the sachem. In Needham the sachem's name was Nahatan (also written as Nehoiden or as William Hahaton). Dedham bought the great plain that became Needham from Nahatan in April, 1680. He retained forty acres at Upper Falls, where there was a weir just below the falls for catching fish and eels. Dedham used the "great plain" for growing grain crops, but few families lived on the left bank of the Charles. When Needham was incorporated in 1711 it still had a scanty population. It was named for a town that neighbored old England's Dedham.

In the middle 1600s a sachem named Noanet lived in southern Needham in what is now called Charles River Village. Noanet's wigwam was on a hillside on the north bank of the Charles, and his people set weirs in the mouth of Dover's Noanet Brook. Because a steep drop in the river made water power available, commercial mill operations at Charles River Village began as early as 1796 in the form of a paper mill. After 1862 one mill made shoddy (an inexpensive fabric of recycled wool) and a second mill made manila paper, but both burned in 1883. Water power was used at Charles River Village by the Needham Tire Company from 1904 through 1918, and subsequently until 1933 by a textile manufacturer named J.E. Cochrane and Son.

The Charles River Railroad opened to Needham in June of 1853. Beginning in 1858 this railroad transported gravel to fill Boston's Back Bay. The source of the gravel was hills at East Needham, south of Upper Falls, near the Charles. In the course of this operation, which continued into the early 1870s, hundreds of acres were leveled.

Wellesley

For most of its history Wellesley was Needham's West Precinct. The part of Wellesley that now has the Hunnewell Mansion and the south entrance to the Wellesley College campus was originally within the bounds of the Indian town of Natick. John Eliot, the Indian's minister, doubled as their chief engineer. He helped them build a sawmill on what is now called Waban Brook.

In about 1681 Wellesley Hills was purchased from an Indian named Magus. During King Philip's War, Magus had been transported to Deer Island in Boston Harbor, along with the other Christian Indians. In the spring of 1676 Magus was made lieutenant of a company of Indians who fought on the side of the English. Their assistance was considered an important factor in Philip's defeat. After the war, Magus was a teacher at Natick. He spent much of his time at Hemlock Gorge, following Nahatan in occupancy there.

Because the series of rapids called Lower Falls offered a good supply of water power, a complex of industries developed there. Benjamin Mills had a grist mill in 1678. In 1703 John Hubbard bought land and built a forge and ironworks. The first paper mill was built around 1790; paper making became the main industry. By 1816 Lower Falls industries included two paper mills, four snuff mills, a tannery, forge shop, fulling mill, wire and screw factory, nail works, blacksmithie, rolling mill, sawmill, cotton and clothing mills, machine shops, and two hotels. In 1824, mill laborers worked from 5:00 a.m. until 7:00 p.m., with thirty minutes for breakfast and forty-five minutes for dinner. In 1918 four water wheels were still in use for making pressboard paper. During the 1920s water power was finally abandoned. Some of the old fieldstone buildings are still in use, and the area retains its industrial character.

Wellesley Hills was at first called Nehoiden. When the Boston and Worcester Railroad began service in June of 1834, it was called Grantville. It has been Wellesley Hills since 1881. The railroad's passage through West Needham gave the area a big advantage as a bedroom community. By 1881, when Wellesley finally gained independence from Needham (on its seventeenth attempt), Boston commuters had five stations in Wellesley, and it was larger in population than its parent town.

Dover and Westwood
Dedham settlers referred to the area that became Dover as "Springhill" and "Springfield" because there were many springs there. Noanet's occupation of Charles River Village spilled across to eastern Dover, which included the Noanet Valley and Noanet's Brook.

Dover was settled around 1700, and set off from Dedham in 1749. Ephraim Wilson took land near the

Dedham line, and Samuel Chickering settled at Powisset near "Rattlesnake Rock." Rattlesnakes survived in troublesome numbers until the 1760s. They were hunted for their oil, which was used for rheumatism and sprains.

The Charles River winds around Dover for two miles. Without turnpikes, railroads, or waterpower, Dover remained agricultural. There are falls at South Natick, but both banks there had been reserved for the Indians and remained part of Natick. Another fall is at Charles River Village, but most of the development was on the Needham side. In 1897 Dover had only 147 houses, and its economy was based on dairy farming and market gardening. Many of the farms later became country estates.

Westwood's history is similar. It was not set off from Dedham until 1896. Dedham had by this time acquired an urban, industrial character, whereas Westwood was agricultural. The town first chose the name Nahatan after the local sachem, but the citizens of Nahant, a North Shore town, objected that the similarity of names would cause confusion.

Natick

After finding that Nonantum was unsuitable for an Indian town, Waban and John Eliot had to obtain permission for settlement elsewhere. After months of scouting for a favorable location, Natick was agreed upon. The General Court granted the Indians 2,000 acres to the north of the Charles, but the Indians settled on both sides of the river and built a bridge. Dedham sued to evict the Indians from land on the south bank, but the General Court let the Indians stay and gave Dedham 8,000 acres in Deerfield as compensation. Natick still straddles the Charles.

The town was launched in 1651. An Indian family named Speene already lived at Natick. They gave up the land but reserved the use of a weir they had built in the river. Such weirs consisted of two stone walls converging toward the point of a V, where fish were trapped in a cage-like basket. The Speenes stayed in the Indian town, and their descendants were residents for many years. One of modern Natick's heavily travelled streets bears the family name.

The Indians' bridge spanned an eighty-foot river. Its central arch was nine feet high. This footbridge outlasted floods and stood unbroken for many years, to the pride of Indian residents. In his address for the 1901 celebration of Medfield's 250th Anniverary, town historian William Tilden said: "Our earliest bridge over Charles River, a little way above the present poor-farm bridge, was carried away by a freshet; Eliot's Indians had built a bridge at Natick about the same time; and they plumed themselves greatly that their bridge stood, while that at Medfield was washed away."

At first the Indians lived in wigwams. A sawmill was established on Waban Brook and English-style carpentry was begun, but many Indians found wigwams warmer and more comfortable.

John Eliot established the first Natick government along a Biblical plan, using the system given to Moses by Jethro. One man was chosen out of every ten to judge small matters. The heirarchy ascended to leaders of fifty, and to a single patriarch to settle the major disputes. An elderly man named Totherswamp was the highest ruler. Waban was one of the rulers of fifty. A warrant he issued has been preserved: "You big constable, quick you catch him, Jeremiah Offscoe; strong you hold him; safe you bring him afore me. Thomas Waban, Justice Peace."

Whether or not we are sympathetic with John Eliot's efforts to imbue the natives with English culture, the fact that he cared about their welfare makes him stand out, and his gentleness, his incredible energy and diligence, and his loyalty to his converts during King Philip's War mark him as heroic. He was born in August, 1604 at Widford, Hertfordshire, England. He received a degree from Jesus College, Cambridge, in 1622. Puritan friends invited him to move to Massachusetts with them as their minister. Eliot sailed in the ship *Lyon*, and reached Boston in November, 1631 in the company of Governor Winthrop's wife and children. Eliot married Ann Mumford in October of 1632. When his friends from Essex arrived and settled in Roxbury, Eliot joined them. He ministered to their church for nearly sixty years.

In 1641 Eliot hired an Indian named Cockenoe to translate for him and to teach him the Algonquian tongue. On October 28, 1646, he preached at Nonantum, and began his association with Waban's people. News of Eliot's work was published in England, where there was more sympathy with Native Americans than there was in the New

World. In 1649 Parliament created the Society for the
Propagation of the Gospel in New-England. Every house
in England was canvassed, making Eliot famous as "Apostle to the Indians." In the first year, 12,000 pounds was
collected and invested. The income supported Eliot's
work.

At the same time that he was establishing Natick,
Eliot decided that the Indians must have a Bible in their
own language. The fact that this language had never been
written did not discourage him. Eliot devised a phonetic
system for reading and writing Algonquian, and began the
enormous task of translation. His work is a valuable
record for linguists. The *Natick Dictionary*, published in
1903 by the U.S. Government Printing Office, lists many
translations including *umshuu*, a canoe; *paugatemissaund*,
an oak canoe; *wompmissaund,* a chestnut canoe; and
wawaund, a pine canoe.

Eliot's New Testament translation was published in
1661 and the Old Testament in 1663. It was the first Bible
published in North America. Eliot preached at Natick
every other week until he was too feeble from old age to
ride out from Roxbury.

The success of Natick encouraged Eliot and his
associates to create other towns. By 1674 they had
established fourteen towns modelled after Natick, with a
combined population of about 1,100. Eliot's assistant, Daniel
Gookin, was superintendent of all these towns. The
Indian town of Hassanamasitt became Grafton. Okom-
makamesit is now Marlborough, Wamesitt was at Lowell,
Nashobah at Littleton. Magunkaquog became Ashland.
Machage, Chabanakongkowun, Maanexit, and Quantisset
were to the west, in Nipmuck territory. Wabquissit was
seventy-two miles from Boston, but Eliot and Gookin
travelled to each, and made a tour of all fourteen in 1674.
This was a farewell visit, because King Philip's War
brought it all down.

At the time of the war about a quarter of the Indians
were Christian. Another quarter sided with the English.
But as their losses mounted, most whites mistrusted all
natives. Though whites outnumbered the Indians, in the
fall of 1675 the frightened English saw their annihilation
as possible or even probable. The towns of Brookfield,
Dartmouth, Deerfield, Groton, Lancaster, Mendon,
Middleborough, Northfield, Simsbury, Warwick, Wickford,

Worcester, and Wrentham were destroyed. It was not a war of large battles; Philip's forces were guerrilla fighters.

In October of 1675 the praying Indians were removed to Deer Island "For their and our security," according to the order. Eliot wrote that his people were "Harried away to an island at half an hour's warning, poor souls in terror they left their goods, books, Bibles, only some few carried their Bibles; the rest were spoiled and lost. The profane Indians prove a sharp rod to the English, and the English prove a very sharp rod to the praying Indians."

Eliot and Gookin visited Deer Island several times during the winter, and were criticized for remaining friendly with Indians. There were harsh privations on Deer Island, but it might have been much worse for the Indians if they had been closer to the Indian-hating whites. After the burning of Medfield there were calls for the extermination of the Indians on Deer Island. But Eliot's Indians began to serve as messengers and guides. They were taken off the island, armed, and proven trustworthy, and the most violent of the racial hatred abated.

By 1676, at the end of King Philip's War, Eliot was seventy-two, too old to begin again from nothing. The number of Christian Indian towns dropped to four, and in time these dwindled. The surviving Indians returned and rebuilt Natick, which was the only town that kept its Indian name. Natick's church was Indian for twenty-six more years. After 1716 it was an English church with Indians as fellow members. The last Indian officeholder left his position in 1745. By 1764 Natick's sixty-five white families outnumbered the Indians, and by 1787 little land was still in Indian hands.

In February of 1781 the district of Natick was finally made into a town. Most residents lived on Pegan Plain at the center of town. Natick was primarily agricultural until the Boston and Worcester Railroad came through in the 1830s. Boot and shoemaking industries grew up along the railroad, and Natick found a successful mixture of industry and agriculture.

Sherborn and Holliston

Sherborn

Sherborn's first settlers were Nicholas Wood, Thomas
Holbrook, and Andrew Pitcher, who arrived in the early
1650s. It is unlikely that they came alone, but the names
of wives are missing from the histories of Sherborn and
other towns, because the documents used to write the
histories recorded only the men's names. The Holbrooks
settled where the Asa Howe house now stands, and the
Woods three-quarters of a mile to the north, near Rocky
Narrows. Daniel Morse came in 1656. These early settlers
moved from Dorchester and Medfield and Dedham. They
lie in unmarked graves in an old burying ground near the
site of Death's Bridge. Henry Death purchased the
Holbrook Farm, and the nearby bridge came to take his
name, which is sometimes spelled Dearth.

A second contingent of pioneers came in 1658 and settled in the southern end of town at Bogastow (Boggestow,
Bogistow), which is what the Indians called the Charles
Valley from Sherborn south to Medway. One of this
group, George Fairbanks, built a large stone-faced fort at
his farm on South End Pond. Because the pond was eventually determined to lie in the northern part of Millis
instead of the southern end of Sherborn, the story of the
defense of this fort is in the Millis section, on page 193.

Sherborn was recognized as a town in October of
1674, when it had fourteen families. It was spelled Sher-
borne, then Sherburne, and changed to Sherborn in 1852.
It was named for the English home of some of its
pioneers. Daniel Gookin, John Eliot's assistant, was
ordained as minister of Sherborn in March of 1685.

Sherborn's history parallels that of Dover, with which
it now shares a regional high school. Sherborn was not on
an early rail line and did not have water power. It never
became industrial, but remained agricultural. Eventually
its low population density attracted affluent families wishing to establish country estates in tranquil surroundings.

Holliston

The first grant of Holliston land was made in 1659. Part of
it went to Dean Winthrop, son of the governor. That grant
included Holliston's largest body of water, a pond that is
the source of Bogastow Brook and that bears Winthrop's

name, though Winthrop never lived there. A subtribe of the Nipmucks called the Muscksquit had a village at the southern end of this pond, which they referred to as Wennakeening. They grew corn, beans, and squash in nearby fields. The Muscksquit were gone by 1700.

Holliston had few settlers until 1679, when a grant was made for the establishment of a sawmill on Bogastow Brook. Holliston was originally part of Sherborn. When it was set off in 1724, because of the difficulty its citizens had in travelling to meet for worship, Holliston had fewer than 150 residents, thirty houses, and no village center. But eventually the town had an industrial flowering. Holliston's nineteenth-century population peaked between 1850 and 1860, during the period that shoes, thread, straw hats, lace, pumps, blankets, furniture, leather, and iron implements were manufactured in the town.

Medfield, Medway, and Millis
Medfield
Because the meadows of Medfield lay too far to the southwest of Dedham Center for convenience, Dedham decided to found a new town. The land on the west side of the Charles was still held by the Commonwealth as "country land." In 1649 it was granted to Dedham for incorporation into the new town, which was set off from Dedham in 1650 with the active cooperation of the parent town. Medfield was probably chosen as the name of the new town because Dedham and Wrentham were near Medfield in old England. Ralph Wheelock is considered the founder of Medfield, but Thomas Wight and Robert Hinsdell were also in the first group of settlers. In 1650 the founding committee established rules for the apportioning of land:

> It is ordered that no house-lot shall exceed twelve acres of upland and twelve acres of meadow, neither shall any houselot be less than six acres of upland and six acres of meadow; and any man's estate shall receive land according to its apportion between these sums, according to what their persons and estates are capable of.
>
> (from *History of Medfield* by William S. Tilden, 1887)

The pioneers began to build the town in May, 1651. The Charles was bridged by 1653. The town's first wedding took place in 1656, when Thomas Holbrook married Hannah Sheppard. In 1658 Medfield awarded its selectmen one free dinner as their compensation, and paid twenty shillings to someone for sweeping out the meetinghouse and for beating the drum to summon the congregants. There was a period in which canoes were regulated.

In 1661 the selectmen passed a restriction on boating:

> Many people through the country had been drowned by means of canoes; and, as a precaution, no person in this town was to make or to have any canoe, in any pond, brook, or river, except allowed by the selectmen, under penalty of 10 shilling fine.

(from *History of Medfield* by William S. Tilden, 1887)

By the time war broke out, Medfield was well established. The town straddled the Charles; its lands to the west of the river were joined to the village by the "Great Bridge" which was near today's West Street Bridge. In 1675 relations between the English and the Indians collapsed and the Wampanoag sachem Metacomet, or Philip, led an attempt to extinguish the Massachusetts Bay Colony. For years tension had increased, because the English had displaced the natives on more and more land. The violence began in June when a Wampanoag friendly to the whites was murdered. Three of Philip's men were accused of the killing and were executed. Confident of easy victory, the colonists planned for war, and some with eyes on Indian land probably welcomed the chance to strike at the Wampanoag and Narragansett. After Philip attacked Swansea and Mendon in July of 1675, fighting swirled through Massachusetts bringing disaster for whites and Indians alike.

Because outlying towns were abandoned after Indian raids, Medfield felt increasingly exposed. In February of 1676 Medfield's minister wrote to the Governor and Council requesting reinforcements. Governor Leverett sent eighty men. The expected attack came a week later, on Monday, February 21, 1676. Half of the town's one hundred houses were burned, along with two mills. Seventeen settlers were killed, including two of the founders, Henry Adams and Timothy Dwight, but the center of the town was saved. Besides its garrison of soldiers, the village had a cannon, which was fired to signal Dedham. After the second firing of the gun, the Indians crossed the Charles River, some at the Great Bridge and some at the bridge to Sherborn that later became known as Death's Bridge. To discourage pursuit, the Indians

fired the bridges. On the ruins at Death's Bridge they left
this notice:

> Know by this paper that the Indians that thou has pro-
> voked to wrath and anger will war these twenty-one years,
> if you will. There are many Indians yet. We come three
> hundred at this time. You must consider that the Indians
> loose nothing but their lives, you must loose your fair
> houses and cattle.
>
> (from *History of Medfield*
> by William S. Tilden, 1887)

This is thought to have been written by an Indian
called James-the-printer who had been educated by the
whites, apprenticed to a printer, and had run away to join
Philip when the war began.

Having depleted the food resources of the villages
they captured, finding their own towns and crops burned
by their enemy, running short of ammunition, and beset
by Mohawks from the west, Philip's warriors dispersed or
surrendered the following summer, and Philip was killed
in August. Massachusetts and Plymouth had lost 600 people, fifty towns, and much livestock. The bitterness of the
colonies was tempered only slightly by the assistance
they had from some of the Christian Indians. Most of the
captives were executed or sold into slavery in the West
Indies. The Indians' losses were about 3000, approximately one-third of their population, including many non-
combatants. Because some Puritan leaders sought to
eliminate the Wampanoags and Narragansetts, their
policy did not spare civilians.

Medfield recovered slowly from the war. In 1713,
when Medway separated its fifty households from Medfield, the parent town was left with only ninety-four
families, but gradually both towns increased. Medfield's
last bear was killed about 1730; its last moose in 1745.

Medfield became involved in another conflict, less
deadly than King Philip's War but longer lasting. The
town voted to ask the General Court to prohibit Thomas
Sawin from damming the Charles at Natick. In 1723,
Sawin was compelled to remove a dam that reduced
drainage of the meadows. In 1743 owners of meadows
near Long Causey (as *causeway* was often spelled) com-
plained to the General Court that another dam at Natick
was keeping their meadows under water all year round. A
decade later they sued Mathew Hastings over the same
issue, but lost. In 1795 Governor Adams appointed a com-

mittee to view the Charles from Natick to two miles
above Dwight's Bridge. The committee recommended
that William Bigelow leave the flashboards off the top of
his dam in Natick during seasons of high water. In 1844
the town sued A.C. Curtis and W. Curtis for damages in
"flowing" (flooding) the meadow land by their dam at
Natick. Experts still argue about whether it was dams
that changed the meadows, or whether the systematic
harvesting of hay might have been responsible. On the
Concord River there was an identical dispute between the
mill owners at Billerica and the farmers of Concord and
Sudbury.

The Boston and Hartford Turnpike, built in 1806, was
used by a line of stagecoaches. Drivers approaching Medfield's village center blew a bugle to call for fresh horses.
Construction of the turnpike required an expensive
causeway and a new river bridge. The crossing was
dubbed "The Willows" because of the large black willows
that shaded the causeway. After the turnpike went bankrupt in 1820, the road became a public way; the Medfield part of it is now Route 109. An electric trolley ran
along the road from 1899 to 1924. The big willow trees
were destroyed by the hurricane of 1938.

Medway
Medway separated from Medfield in 1713, and Millis
from Medway in 1885. The land that became Millis was
closer to Medfield's village center and was settled earlier.
It was not until 1700 that Henry Garnsey of Roxbury
became the first settler of Medway. Garnsey married
Sarah Wheelock of Medfield and built a house just east of
Chicken Brook that stood until 1910. Chicken Brook
received its name because a pioneer named Joe Barber
dropped a crate of chickens while fording it, with a disas-
trous result for the poultry. Barber supposedly tried to
charge extra for these chickens because they were
already killed and soaked.

Because the Charles falls almost fifty feet between
West Medway and Populatic Pond, Medway had power for
mills, which are described on page 32. In addition to the
mills, the manufacture of boots and shoes began in 1828
and became a major occupation, with as many as thirteen
shops in town at one time.

The dawn of the railroad era in the 1830s did not
bring any rail lines through Medway. The town's indus-

trialists took action, and sponsored a branch of the Norfolk County Railroad that ended on the east end of town near the Populatic Street Bridge. A little woodburning engine called the Hookset pulled two wooden coaches the day service commenced, in January, 1853. There were speeches by the local dignitaries, nods and bows from the train crew, and the firing of a cannon. For regular service, trains were mixed: engine, tender, boxcar, coach. A crowd of thousands cheered the departure of Medway's Company E of the Massachusetts Volunteers when it departed to join its regiment in West Roxbury in May of 1861. The regiment trained at Brook Farm. This was the line's last passenger traffic; it had never been profitable, and in 1864 it was discontinued and the tracks taken up.

In 1861 trains began running through Medway and West Medway on the Airline Railroad, which became the New York and New England Railroad, Woonsocket Division. Freight service on these tracks continued until the mid-1960s.

By 1900 Medway's industry had declined, and the town was predominantly agricultural until suburban housing developments began to appear in the 1960s, gradually changing the town into a bedroom community.

Millis

George Fairbanks was one of those who took up land at "Boggestow Farms" in 1658. His friends are numbered among Sherborn's pioneers, but Fairbanks' farm was south of the boundary between Sherborn and Millis when that line was established, so Fairbanks is remembered as the first English occupant of Millis. Perhaps because of his isolation from the village at Medfield, Fairbanks built his house of stone. His garrison was on the north shore of South End Pond. It was sixty-five feet long and two stories high. Some of the stones were still visible in 1836, but the last of them had been hauled off by 1886, and for a century no one has known exactly where Fairbanks' house stood.

When the Indians attacked Medfield on February 21, 1676, nine families took refuge in the stone house. All were from the west side of the river; half were from Sherborn and half from Millis; over sixty people in all. An elderly man who was too feeble to go there perished in the flames of his home. Those within Fairbank's stone house survived the February attack, but during the battle

Jonathan Wood was killed at Death's Bridge. His wife was a mile upstream in the garrison house. When told of his death, she went into labor, bore a daughter, and died hours later. They named the baby Silence. She grew up to marry John Holbrook who had been an infant in the stone house at the time of her birth.

As buildings burned all over Medfield, the Indians gathered at a grove of tupelo trees on a hillside within sight of the town, on the western side of the Great Bridge which they had fired. They roasted an ox. One tale has it that Philip himself galloped back and forth astride a black horse, though historians doubt that he was present. A warrior named Monaco later boasted of having burned Lancaster and Medfield. He was captured and executed at the end of the war.

Fairbank's garrison house was attacked again on May 6, 1676. The Indians attempted to ignite the house by rolling a cart loaded with burning flax down the hill, but the cart lodged on a boulder, and when a warrior attempted to free the cart, he was killed by a shot from the house. Again the attack was resisted successfully. Friendly Indians from Natick were on hand to assist with the defense.

In later years both George Fairbanks and his son Jonathan drowned, on separate occasions, while trying to cross the Charles.

Joseph Daniel was the second white settler of Millis. The house he built in 1676 to replace the one burned by the Indians still stands, overlooking Bogastow Brook. The big barn predates 1660 and is one of the oldest buildings in Millis. It is thought to have been spared by the Indians to repay generosity shown them by the Daniel family.

Medfield's first female school teacher was Experience Adams, who kept a school on the Millis side of the river in 1699.

For many years Millis was East Medway. There were mills at Rockville from the 1680s. When a cotton mill was built there in 1818, the location was known as Rock Bottom. In 1892 the Millis Barge Club built a boat house at the dam. The Rockville Paper Mill burned in 1896. There was also a mill at Baltimore Street (Route 115), called the Baltimore Mill because the first proprietor, Moses Harding, had thought of going to Baltimore before he set up in Millis.

In February of 1885, East Medway was set off and named for Lansing Millis, a wealthy resident.

Wrentham, Bellingham, Franklin, and Norfolk

Wrentham

Dedham's records refer to the owner of the wigwam at Wollomonopoag as George Indian. In 1660 Dedham voted to send a committee to Wollonmonopoag to see about buying the surrounding land. A payment of twenty-four pounds and ten shillings was made, and Dedham thought it had bought Wollomonopoag ("Place of Shells") from its Wampanoag owners. A white named Samuel Sheares settled about 1666, but the Wampanoag sachem, Metacomet, did not consider the title clear. He obtained an additional payment, which was set at seventeen pounds eight pence in November of 1669.

In 1671 Sheares was joined by other settlers. Two years later Wrentham was established as a separate town because it was so far from Dedham. In 1675 Robert Crossman built a mill on the stream that runs out of Wollomonopoag Pond. The name of the pond has been changed to Lake Pearl. The outflowing stream is called Eagle Brook in its upper half, but in Norfolk it becomes Mill River.

Indians were numerous cohabitants in Wrentham's earliest years, and relations were so amicable that the whites remained safely in their isolated outpost through most of King Philip's War. Though the fighting had started the previous summer, Wrentham was not abandoned until March of 1676, after the attack on Medfield. Subsequently, all but two of the empty houses were burned; these two were thought by the Indians to have been infected with smallpox, and they were avoided altogether.

Wrentham was resettled in 1680. In 1703, town father Samuel Sheares was voted exempt from taxes. The pace of settlement quickened. In 1718 Wrentham had four districts, one to the north of the central village and two lying westward. These districts became the towns of Norfolk, Bellingham, and Franklin. Wrentham never had much industry. There were agricultural enterprises such as poultry farms, but the town has been basically residential in character.

Bellingham

The first of Wrentham's offspring was Bellingham, which was named for Richard Bellingham, the third governor of

Massachusetts. A Dedham committee visited this most western precinct in 1695 and gave a negative report on the fertility of the area. Farmers sometimes ventured to the Bellingham Meadows to cut hay. It was so far from the beaten path that the first whites who wished to live there were those whose religious views differed from Puritan orthodoxy and who were therefore happier living out of the government's reach. The first settler was a Quaker, Jacob Bartlett of Providence, who took up residence in 1698. He was eventually imprisoned in Boston for refusing to support the town church. The second pioneer was Nicholas Cook, a Baptist. Conventional Congregationalists came too, and the town was set off and incorporated in May of 1719.

For its first century nearly all of Bellingham's people were farmers, but the Charles River has good falls in Bellingham and the power available was well suited to the technology of the 1800s. The most upstream of the mill sites was at the point where the Charles enters Bellingham, at the village of South Milford. A woolen mill built here in 1812 became known as the Eagle Mill. In 1837 it had two sets of machinery and made 24,000 yards of cloth per year. Moses Whiting took possession in 1840 and ran it as the Bellingham Woolen Mill until 1859. In 1864, the Thayer and Sweet firm of Hopkinton made flannels there. The Eagle Mill burned in 1868 and was not rebuilt, but remnants of the stone walls stood for years. Its dam held Factory Pond as late as 1919.

Box Pond was providing water for a sawmill by 1783. In 1830 there were corn and sawmills at its outflow. In 1863 the Ray family bought these mills, gained the right to flood the area that is the Box Pond of today, and increased the dam's height accordingly.

Textile manufacture began at Charles River Grove in the 1830s, in what was known as the Red Mill. In the same era the White and Yellow Mills were in operation downstream in Medway. The Red Mill burned in 1909, and the dam was breached by a flood in 1927.

A cotton mill was built at North Bellingham in 1810 by Joseph Ray. In 1839 it was bought by Bates and Arnold. By 1884 it was a satinet mill with 150 employees. At the end of the century it became a woolen mill. In 1919 it was operated by the Bellingham Woolen Company, which used two steam boilers and electricity in addition to the water power. The company had forty-nine tenements, a boarding house, and a moving picture hall. During World War I the mill made silk yarn for powder bags. In 1920, fifteen-year-old Sophia Nadolni began work here as a weaver making fabric for mackinaw jackets for fifty cents an hour. At first she was ill at ease, a Polish girl in an Irish town, but she married a fellow named Walter Lewinski who had a good job at the mill as a "dresser and tender." He later served Bellingham as a selectman for sixteen years. Today Sophia Lewinski lives near her former workplace, on the right bank of the river, in a house purchased from the mill owners.

About 1875, John Metcalf built the first mills at Cary-ville, Bellingham's northernmost village. Until 1866, the village of Caryville was called Fairbanks, because Joseph Fairbanks had run mills here since 1800. He was a descendant of George Fairbanks, the first settler of Millis, whose stone palisade sheltered his neighbors during King Philip's War. In 1839 George Barber of Medway bought this mill. Barber's son-in-law, William H. Cary, became the dominant industrialist of the neighborhood, and his name finally replaced Fairbanks as the name of the village. In 1864 Cary sold to the Ray family and moved to Rockville.

Franklin

In 1713 a partnership agreed to build a sawmill on Mine Brook. Modern canoeists find suggestive traces of small scale industry along this brook. After Bellingham had been set off, the area that became Franklin was Wrentham's West Precinct. The West Precinct became independent in 1778, while Benjamin Franklin was representing the new United States in France, and the town chose to take his name. Franklin later donated 116 books to the town.

In 1839 Joseph Ray began the manufacture of cotton goods in Franklin, and by 1884 the town had seven mills. The Milford and Franklin Railroad was completed in 1883. This connected to the Milford and Hopkinton Railroad, which passed near Echo Lake, source of the Charles, and joined the Boston and Albany at Ashland.

Norfolk

Norfolk was the last of Wrentham's districts to form a separate town. When it did so, Wrentham lost its direct contact with the Charles River, though it remained the source of a sizable tributary, Mill River.

Wrentham's North Parish formed because of an intense and long-lasting theological dispute within the town. Those loyal to the preaching of Reverend David Avery broke with the Wrentham church and built a meeting house in about 1796, but the North Parish did not become a separate town until 1870. At that time it received some additional land from the towns of Franklin, Medway, and Walpole.

Mill River began turning grindstones at City Mills in 1693. By the mid-1800s a complex of mills had grown below the dam. In 1884 the specialty was felt, and there were eighty employees, but otherwise Norfolk remained an agricultural community.

Mendon, Milford, and Hopedale

Mendon

Quinshipaug (Pickerel Pond) was the Indian name for the Mendon area. It was purchased in 1667 from some of the Natick Indians by residents of Braintree and Weymouth. John Eliot witnessed the conveyance. Peter Brackett and Moses Payne were the first settlers in the new town, which was named after the English town of Mendham.

Mendon was the first of the Massachusetts Bay Colony towns to be attacked during King Philip's War. On July 14, 1675, Nipmucks killed five or six settlers. The surviving English fled the new town. All of its buildings were burned before the end of the war. By 1680 twenty families were back in town, including Reverend Grindal Rawson, who served as pastor until 1715. Rawson learned the Algonquian language. He was granted a large farm in 1685, in the part of Mendon that became the northwest corner of Bellingham.

In 1701 William Holbrook claimed the last bounty Mendon paid on wolves. He had killed five.

The original Mendon was a great tract of land. The parent ceded its lands to offspring communities gradually and grudgingly. Bellingham took a piece of Mendon in 1719. Uxbridge took another in 1727, and Upton had some in 1735. Milford received a large area in 1780, and in 1845 some went to Blackstone. What was left of Mendon had an industrial flowering in the mid-1800s, but because the railroads bypassed the town and it lacked waterpower, factories moved elsewhere and Mendon reverted to agriculture.

Milford and Hopedale

Mendon's East Precinct sought separation as early as 1727 and finally was set off as Milford in 1780. Present-day Hopedale was included within its boundaries.

At its northern end Milford has a natural resource, the beautiful speckled pink rock called Milford granite. The uppermost Charles winds between outcrops of Milford granite. It was quarried in a small way before it could be hauled out by train, but the construction of the Hopkinton and Milford Railroad, chartered in 1867, opened the way for large-scale operations. Railroad sidings served four quarries: the Fletcher Quarry, the Massachusetts Pink Granite Company, the George H. Cutting Quarry, and the Bay State Quarry. In 1875 the quarries employed 200 workers in Milford.

Milford granite was used extensively in the construction of the Boston Public Library in 1888. When a major addition was built in the 1970s, the quarry was reopened to supply additional stone. In the 1880s Milford granite was built into stations of the Boston and Albany Railroad at Newton Centre, Chestnut Hill, Wellesley Hills, Framingham, and Ashland. In this era the stone could be carried by rail from the quarries, on tracks that curved through Hopkinton to a junction with the main line of the Boston and Albany at Ashland. An enormous pillar was cut from a single block of stone for shipment to Cleveland for the Ohio Citizen's Bank. The pillar was twenty-eight feet long and four feet, nine inches in diameter.

Inspired by the Transcendentalist movement, a Unitarian minister named Adin Ballou initiated the formation of the Hopedale Community. In January of 1841, thirty-two individuals signed its constitution. It was a "joint stock and united industrial association." In the 1840s at least sixty communities around the country were trying to find a form of group living that would succeed in improving society. Ballou and his associates were impatient with the progress of the established church in reform.

> Even the more advanced classes in church and state, seeking the progress, the harmony, and happiness of mankind, propose little if anything more than the *gradual improvement* of society on the old basis of egoism, caste distinctions, competitive rivalry, shrewd and cunning practices, jealousy and hatred of race and nation.
>
> (from Adin Ballou's *The Hopedale Community*, 1876)

Ballou's "practical Christian Socialism" had 200 prac-
titioners. The Hopedale Community outlived Brook Farm,
survived the 1840s, and was prosperous in 1854, but
bankrupt two years later. The community's assets were
purchased by Ebenezer and George Draper, who had
been involved in its finances. The Draper Company did
well producing machinery for milling cotton, and Ballou's
group continued as a religious society until 1867. Ballou
authored a history of the Hopedale Community and a history of Milford, and lived in Hopedale until his death in
1890 at the age of 87.

In April of 1886, at the instigation of George Draper,
Hopedale separated from Milford.

Hopkinton

Magunkaquog, the seventh of the Indian towns founded
by John Eliot, was the home of eleven native families in
1670. The town's name was also written as Moguncoy,
Magunkayoog, Magunkayog, and Wagwonkkommonk.
After King Philip's War it combined with Natick.

The first white settlers arrived about 1710. The
Magunkaquog lands were purchased from the Indians by
the trustees of the Edward Hopkins legacy who were
instructed to invest in New England land, the income to
benefit Harvard College. In 1715 the Hopkins trustees
successfully petitioned the General Court for the creation
of the town of Hopkinton.

At its founding, Hopkinton was bounded by Mendon,
Sherborn, and the Sudbury River. Half of the new town's
farmland was leased to tenants for terms of ninty-nine
years and the remainder was set aside for common use.
When the leases expired, the legislature bought the rights
of the trustees for $8,000, and Harvard and Hopkinton
parted ways.

Eighteen Scots-Irish families settled in Hopkinton in
1719, including Joseph Young, ancestor of Mormon founder Brigham Young. The first town meeting was in 1724.
In 1816 mineral springs were discovered west of Lake
Whitehall, and Hopkinton was for a time a fashionable
resort. In 1846 part of Hopkinton was given to the new
town of Ashland. In the 1840s and 1850s Hopkinton had a
successful boot and shoe industry. Its population grew
during this industrial period, cresting at 4,340 in 1860 and
declining as manufacturing tapered off after 1880.

The Hopkinton and Milford Railroad was chartered in 1867. Its grade is visible where it crosses Hayden Row Street (Route 85) at the boundary with Milford. Originally, the railroad made a circuit of Hopkinton and joined the Boston and Albany at Ashland. Long after the tracks to Ashland had been taken up, freight deliveries continued to Hopkinton through Milford. The end came in the 1950s, when a bridge at Milford Pond was washed out and was not replaced.

Hopkinton is at the headwaters of three rivers. Its western edge drains into the upper Blackstone River. Lake Whitehall and its outlet, Whitehall Brook, are important sources of the Sudbury River. And, from the southern side of Hopkinton's central hill, the Charles begins its descent to the sea.

Appendix 1
Suggested Outings Directory

Walks

MILFORD — Those charmed by the natural sculptures of ledge outcrops will enjoy visiting the terrain around the upper Charles, where Milford granite is at or near the surface. See "Walk to Echo Lake," page 10.

BELLINGHAM — An old railroad grade affords a walk along the bank of the upper Charles. See "The abandoned grade," page 35.

MEDWAY — Visit the remains of the Eaton and Wilson Wadding Mill. See "Explore the site," page 35.

MEDFIELD — View the marsh along the Charles from Dwight's Causeway. See "Visit the river meadows," page 57.

MEDFIELD — Ramble in The Trustees of Reservations' Noon Hill Reservation. See "Hike to the summit," page 65.

SHERBORN — The vista from the crest of King Philip's Lookout is worth some effort to reach. See "Hike to King Philip's Lookout," page 71.

DOVER — Peters Reservation, one of several Trustees of Reservations properties on the Charles, offers excellent foot trails. See "The Peters Reservation," page 80.

NATICK — In terms of wildlife habitats, Broadmoor Wildlife Sanctuary has much to offer: woods, fields, ponds, and the river. See "The Charles River Trail," page 80.

DOVER — Enjoy the trails at Elm Bank, which was once a private estate. See "Elm Bank provides ideal walking," page 92.

WELLESLEY — The upper surface of the Sudbury Aqueduct makes a good trail to the top of Waban Arches, from which there is a splendid view. See "Walk to Waban Arches," page 102.

WESTWOOD — Hale Reservation and the Noanet Woodlands have an extensive trail system. See "There is great walking," page 107.

WEST ROXBURY — The site of an idealistic community of the 1840s, Brook Farm is worth a visit, especially for admirers of the Transcendentalists. See "Explore Brook Farm," page 113.

NEEDHAM — Cutler Park has good trails. See "Hike the 1.7 mile loop," page 123.

NEEDHAM-NEWTON — Echo Bridge, the Silk Mill, Roxbury conglomerate, and a nice stand of hemlocks all adorn Hemlock Gorge. See "Explore Hemlock Gorge Reservation," page 123.

NEWTON — The foot trail between Quinobequin Road and the river makes it possible to walk between Upper Falls and Lower Falls. See "Walk along the right bank," page 123.

WESTON-WALTHAM-NEWTON — Ambitious hikers can walk all the way around the Lakes District and stay at or near the Charles most of the journey. See "Hike around," page 133.

WALTHAM — The Charles River Museum of Industry has exhibits about textile mills and other manufacturing in this region. See "Visit the Charles River Museum of Industry," page 140.

WATERTOWN — A narrow park along the Charles invites pedestrians. See "Walk along the left bank," page 202.

CAMBRIDGE-BOSTON — The universities and parks along the Basin offer excellent urban walking. To visit the Esplanade, see "The south and east shores," page 157.

Canoe Outings

BELLINGHAM — The upper Charles boasts many birds and other wildlife. Variable distance. See "The Bellingham Meadows study area," page 23.

BELLINGHAM — The banks are wooded on this part of the upper Charles. Variable distance. See "Explore upstream from Caryville," page 24.

MEDWAY-FRANKLIN — The scenery is pleasing and the canoeing is easy in the valley between Medway and Franklin. Variable distance. See "Paddle upstream from the Sanford Mill," page 35.

NORFOLK — Paddle the still water of Populatic Pond, then explore the channels from which the Charles enters and leaves the pond. A good outing for beginners. Variable distance. See "Explore Populatic Pond," page 44.

NORFOLK — In high water it is fun to explore a tributary stream called Mill River. Variable distance (up to 4.2 miles). See "Paddle up Mill River," page 50.

MEDWAY-MILLIS-NORFOLK — This outing, more suitable for experienced canoeists than for beginners, mixes nature with some fast-water excitement. Distance: 6.0 miles. See "A downstream trip," page 56.

MILLIS-NORFOLK — Between Millis and Norfolk the Charles passes through pristine woodlands. Variable distance (up to 3.0 miles). See "Paddle upstream," page 65.

MILLIS-MEDFIELD — For ideal recreational canoeing, go to
the heart of the Charles, beginning with the Stop River Confluence section. Distance: 4.6 miles. See "A downstream run,"
page 56.

MILLIS-MEDFIELD — Birders and botanists should visit this
part of the Natural Valley Storage Project. Variable distance.
See "Explore the Stop River Study Area," page 56.

MEDFIELD — A tributary stream called Stop River is well
worth exploring early in the season when the water is high and
the duckweed is low. Variable distance (up to 8.2 miles). See
"Upstream and back," page 65.

MEDFIELD-MILLIS-SHERBORN — Conservation land and
estates along the banks make this section deservedly popular
with canoeists. Distance: 5.3 miles. See "Canoe downstream
from Old Bridge Street," page 70.

MEDFIELD-MILLIS — South End Pond was the site of a
dramatic skirmish during King Philip's War. A visit to the pond
makes a nice outing for anyone, including families and beginners. Distance: 3.2 miles. See "South End Pond," page 71.

MILLIS — Bogastow Brook, the Charles' largest tributary,
offers a nice challenge when there is enough water. Variable
distance (up to 3.5 miles). See "Paddle upstream from South
End Pond," page 75.

SHERBORN-DOVER — Rocky Narrows is picturesque, and the
view is great from King Philip's Lookout. This outing is good for
beginners and families. Variable distance. See "Paddle to Rocky
Narrows," page 71.

SHERBORN-DOVER-NATICK — Float through Broadmoor
Wildlife Sanctuary and into South Natick on a gentle and
beautiful section of the river. This outing is suitable for beginners. Distance: 3.5 miles. See "Canoe downstream," page 79.

NATICK — Broadmoor can be visited from an access point just
below the sanctuary. Variable distance. See "From Eliot Street,"
page 71.

NATICK-DOVER-NEEDHAM — A unique combination of
residential architecture and nature characterize the Bays
Region. Distance: 6.7 miles. See "On a downstream trip," page
91.

DOVER-WELLESLEY — Families and novices can get the feel
of gently moving water in this beautiful, forested area. Variable
distance. See "Explore Elm Bank," page 92.

NEEDHAM-DEDHAM — Savor the meanders of the Dedham Loop, an area rich in wildlife. Distance: 4.6 miles. See "Make the downstream run," page 107, or "Visit Dedham Loop," page 113.

NEEDHAM-NEWTON — The slack current along Cutler Park is a good place for beginners to learn to steer a canoe. Distance: variable. See "Paddle through Cutler Park," page 113.

NEEDHAM-DEDHAM-NEWTON — This long, portage-free trip takes in the whole Dedham Loop. Distance: 9.2 miles. See: "Canoe downstream from South Street," page 113.

WESTON-NEWTON-WALTHAM — Canoes can be rented at waterside for use on the Lakes District, where courtship canoeing is a tradition. Variable distance. See "Explore the Lakes District," or "Make the downstream run," page 132.

ALLSTON-WATERTOWN — There is good canoeing on the upper Basin. Variable distance. See "From Herter Park," page 146, or "Canoe downstream to Captain's Island," page 146.

CAMBRIDGE-BOSTON — For a unique perspective on these cities, paddle the Charles River Basin. Variable distance. See "Explore the Basin," page 152, or "Visit the Esplanade's lagoons," page 157.

Appendix 2

Dams and Bridges on the Charles River

The mileages indicated represent distances downriver from Echo Lake Dam, in Hopkinton. They are derived from river mileages published by the United States Army Corps of Engineers and by the Massachusetts Department of Environmental Protection, with interpolations measured on United States Geological Survey maps.

The Charles is often said to be eighty miles long, which is the distance between the source of Echo Lake's longest tributary brook and the Charles River Dam. As Thoreau notes in the journal passage quoted on page 167, rivers are of indefinite length. The designation of exact points of origin and completion is arbitrary.

The total fall of the Charles is 354 feet, it drains a watershed of 307 square miles, and its average discharge at Waltham is 303 cubic feet per second.

Dams
mile
- 0.0 Echo Lake Dam, Hopkinton
- 1.2 Wildcat Pond Dam, Milford (Waterworks Dam)
- 2.4 Dilla Street Dam, Milford
- 3.4 Milford Pond Dam, Milford (Cedar Swamp Dam)
- 6.8 Factory Pond Dam, Mendon — Bellingham (breached)
- 8.5 Box Pond Dam, Bellingham
- 9.5 Red Mill Dam, Bellingham (breached)
- 12.9 North Bellingham Dam, Bellingham
- 13.9 Caryville Dam, Bellingham
- 16.0 West Medway Dam, Medway — Franklin
- 17.8 Medway Dam, Medway — Franklin
- 21.9 Rockville Dam, Millis — Norfolk (breached)
- 37.8 South Natick Dam, Natick
- 44.4 Cochrane Dam, Dover — Needham
- 58.4 Silk Mill Dam, Needham — Newton
- 58.7 Circular Dam, Needham — Newton
- 60.6 Cordingly Dam, Wellesley — Newton
- 60.9 Finlay Dam, Wellesley — Newton (Lower Falls Dam)
- 66.3 Moody Street Dam, Waltham
- 67.3 Bleachery Dam, Waltham
- 68.5 Bemis Dam, Newton — Watertown (breached) (also called Rolling Stone Dam)
- 69.3 Watertown Dam, Watertown
- 77.7 Science Park Dam, Boston (Charles River Dam of 1910)
- 78.2 Charles River Dam, Boston

Bridges
mile
- 0.8 Cedar Street (Route 85), Milford
- 1.3 Cedar Street (Route 85), Milford
- 2.1 Route 495
- 2.4 Dilla Street, Milford
- 3.6 East Main Street (Route 16), Milford
- 4.0 Central Street, Milford
- 4.9 Railroad
- 5.0 Howard Street, Milford
- 5.7 Howard Street, Hopedale
- 5.9 Mellen Street, Hopedale — Bellingham
- 6.9 Hartford Avenue, Mendon — Bellingham
- 8.7 Depot Street, Bellingham
- 8.8 Railroad
- 9.1 North Main Street (Route 126), Bellingham
- 11.1 High Street, Bellingham
- 11.9 Route 495
- 12.9 Maple Street, Bellingham

13.4 Plymouth Road, Bellingham
13.9 Pearl Street, Bellingham
15.6 Franklin Street, Medway — Pond Street, Franklin
16.2 Private bridge, Medway
16.5 Shaw Street, Medway — Elm Street, Franklin
17.8 Sanford Street, Medway — Lincoln Street, Franklin
18.4 Populatic Street (Walker Street), Medway (Red Bridge)
21.5 Myrtle Street, Millis — Norfolk
21.9 Dean Street — Pleasant Street, Millis
22.9 Baltimore Street (Route 115), Millis
24.4 Forest Road, Millis — Orchard Street, Norfolk
27.9 Main Street (Route 109), Millis — Medfield
29.0 Dover Road, Millis — West Street, Medfield
       (Great Bridge, Brastow's Bridge, Poor Farm Bridge)
31.8 Main Street, Sherborn — Hospital Road, Medfield
       (Route 27) (replaced Death's Bridge)
32.2 Railroad
34.3 Farm Road, Sherborn — Bridge Street, Dover
37.3 Sargent Footbridge, Natick
37.8 Pleasant Street, Natick
38.6 Cheney Bridge, Natick — Dover
40.9 Dover Road, Dover — Charles River Street, Needham
43.6 Centre Street, Dover — Central Avenue, Needham
43.8 Railroad
44.5 **Willow Street, Dover — South Street, Needham**
45.9 Chestnut Street, Dover — Needham
47.4 Dedham Avenue, Needham — Needham Avenue,
       Dedham
48.2 Lyons Street, Dedham — Greendale Avenue, Needham
48.3 **Route 128 (I-95)**
51.7 Bridge Street (Route 109), Dedham
52.1 Ames Street, Dedham
53.6 Bridge Street (Route 109), Dedham — West Roxbury
56.7 Kendrick Street, Needham — Nahanton Street, Newton
57.4 Railroad
57.6 Highland Avenue, Needham — Needham Street, Newton
57.9 Railroad
58.5 **Elliot Street, Newton — Central Avenue, Needham**
58.7 Echo Bridge
58.9 Boston-Worcester Turnpike (Route 9)
60.2 Route 128 (I-95)
60.3 Cochituate Aqueduct
60.6 Water Street, Wellesley — Newton
61.0 Washington Street (Route 16), Wellesley — Newton
62.0 Park Road, Weston — Concord Street, Newton
62.6 Route 128 (I-95)

62.7 Highway access ramp
62.9 Riverside footbridge
63.0 Railroad
63.1 Riverside footbridge
63.2 Massachusetts Turnpike and ramps
63.4 Commonwealth Avenue (Route 30)
65.8 Prospect Street, Waltham
66.3 Moody Street, Waltham
66.5 Railroad
66.5 Landry Park Footbridge
66.7 Newton Street, Waltham
67.0 Railroad
67.1 Footbridge
67.6 Farwell Street, Waltham
68.5 Bridge Street, Newton — Watertown
69.2 Thompson Footbridge
69.5 Galen Street, Watertown
70.9 North Beacon Street (Route 20), Watertown — Boston
71.7 Arsenal Street, Watertown — Boston
72.9 Eliot Bridge, Cambridge — Boston
73.7 Anderson Bridge, Cambridge — Boston
73.9 Weeks Footbridge
74.3 Western Avenue, Cambridge — Boston
74.5 River Street, Cambridge — Boston
75.3 Boston University Bridge, Cambridge — Boston
75.3 Railroad
76.2 Harvard Bridge, Cambridge — Boston
77.3 Longfellow Bridge, Cambridge — Boston
77.7 MBTA Green Line and the O'Brien Highway (Route 28)
77.9 Railroad drawbridge
78.1 Fitzgerald Expressway (Routes 93 and 1)
78.3 Charlestown Bridge, Charlestown — Boston

Appendix 3

Natural Valley Storage Areas

The Natural Valley Storage Project uses the water holding capacities of wetlands to control flooding. For more information, see page 24.

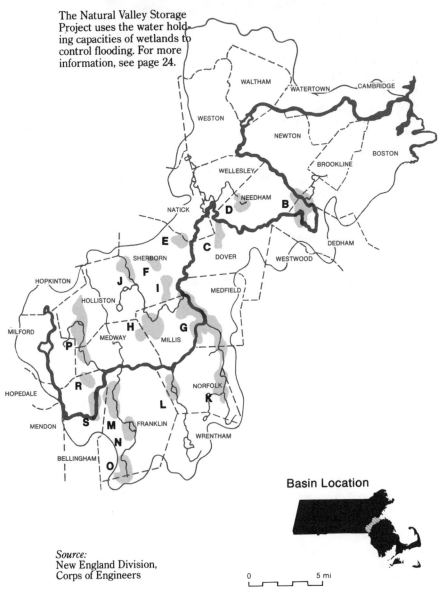

Basin Location

Source:
New England Division,
Corps of Engineers

0   5 mi

Appendix 4
Canoe Training and Boat Liveries

Canoe training is available from:
- Appalachian Mountain Club, 5 Joy Street, Boston, Massachusetts, 02108, (617) 523-0636.
- Charles River Canoe & Kayak Center, 2401 Commonwealth Avenue, Newton, Massachusetts, 02166, (617) 965-5110.
- Outdoor Center of New England, 8 Pleasant Street, Miller's Falls, Massachusetts, 01349, (413) 659-3926.

Canoes can be purchased or rented from many boat and outdoor recreation equipment suppliers in Greater Boston. On the banks of the Charles River canoes can be rented from:

- Charles River Canoe & Kayak Center, 2401 Commonwealth Avenue, Newton, Massachusetts, 02166, (617) 965-5110.
- Upriver Outfitters, 825 Main Street (Route 109), Millis, Massachusetts, (508) 376-1288.

On the Charles River Basin, members of a public sailing club called Community Boating can rent sailboats and windsurfers. For information constact Community Boating at 21 Embankment Road, Boston, Massachusetts, 02114, (617) 523-1038.

BIBLIOGRAPHY

Arrow Publishing Company. *Atlas 1200* Taunton: Arrow Publishing Company, 1983.

Ballou, Adin. *History of the Hopedale Community.* Lowell: Thompson & Hill, 1897.

Ballou, Adin. *History of the Town of Milford.* Milford: Town of Milford, 1882.

Bell, Pat, and David Wright. *Rocks & Minerals.* New York: Macmillan Publishing Company, 1985.

Bickford, Walter E., and Ute Janik Dymon, Editors. *An Atlas of Massachusetts River Systems.* Amherst: University of Massachusetts Press, 1990.

Cahill, Verna E., Editor. "Natural Resources Plan of Milford," 1976.

Charles River Museum of Industry. *Historic Industrial Waltham.* Waltham: Charles River Museum of Industry, 1986.

Clarke, George Kuhn. *History of Needham, Massachusetts.* Cambridge: University Press, 1912.

Conklin, Edwin P. *Middlesex County and Its People.* New York: Lewis Historical Publishing Company Inc., 1927.

Coolidge, Deborah Percy Dows. *The Story of Sherborn.* 1918.

Curtis, John Gould. *History of the Town of Brookline.* Boston: Houghton Mifflin Company, 1933.

Dincauze, Dena F. *A Preliminary Report on the Charles River Archaeological Survey.* Cambridge: Peabody Museum, 1968.

Donovan, Francis D. *The New Grant: A History of Medway.* Medway: Medway Bicentennial Commission, 1976.

Dwelley, Marilyn J. *Summer & Fall Wildflowers of New England.* Camden, Maine: Down East Enterprise, Inc., 1977.

Eaton, Richard Jefferson. *A Flora of Concord.* Cambridge: Museum of Comparative Zoology, Harvard University, 1974.

Emmet, Alan. Cambridge, Massachusetts: *The Changing of a Landscape.* Cambridge: Harvard University, 1978.

Fiore, Jordan D. *Wrentham 1673-1973, A History.* Wrentham: Town of Wrentham, 1973.

Fiske, Joseph E. *History of the Town of Wellesley, Massachusetts.* Boston: The Pilgrim Press, 1917.

Flood, Richard T. *The Story of Noble and Greenough School.* Dedham: Noble and Greenough School, 1966.

Fleishman, Thelma. *Charles River Dams.* Auburndale: Charles River Watershed Association, 1978.

Forbush, Edward Howe. *Birds of Massachusetts and other New England States, Volume I.* Boston: Commonwealth of Massachusetts, 1925.

Forbush, Edward Howe. *Birds of Massachusetts and other New England States, Volume II.* Boston: Commonwealth of Massachusetts, 1927.

Forbush, Edward Howe. *Birds of Massachusetts and other New England States, Volume III.* Boston: Commonwealth of Massachusetts, 1929.

Giezentanner, William D. *Charles River Pathway Plan.* Newton: Newton Conservation Commission, 1975.

Gadoury, R.A., R.S. Socolow, R.W. Bell, and T.J. Calderini, *Water Resources Data, Massachusetts and Rhode Island, 1988.* Boston: United States Geological Survey, 1990.

Haglund, Karl T. "Boston's Court of Honor: The Almost Foregone Creation of the Charles River Basin". 1987.

Hall, Max. *The Charles.* Boston: Godine, 1986.

Halliwell, David B. *Inventory of Rivers and Streams.* Westborough: Massachusetts Division of Water Pollution Control and Massachusetts Division of Fisheries and Wildlife, 1982.

Hanson, Robert Brand. *Dedham, Massachusetts.* Dedham: Dedham Historical Society, 1976.

Harding, Walter, Editor. *Selections from the Journals of Henry David Thoreau.* Salt Lake City, Utah: Gibbs M. Smith Inc., 1982.

Harlow, Alvin F. *Steelways of New England.* New York: Creative Age Press, 1946.

Hodges, Maud deLeigh. *Crossroads on the Charles.* Canaan, New Hampshire: Phoenix Publishing, 1980.

Hotchkiss, Neil. *Common Marsh, Underwater, & Floating-leaved Plants.* New York: Dover Publications, 1972.

Howe, Henry F. *Salt Rivers of the Massachusetts Shore.* New York: Rinehart and Company, 1951.

Hurd, D. Hamilton, Compiler. *History of Norfolk County.* Philadelphia: J.W. Lewis & Company, 1884.

Jameson, E.O. *The History of Medway, Massachusetts 1713-1785*. Medway: Town of Medway, 1886.

Klots, Elsie B. *The New Field Book of Freshwater Life*. New York: G.P. Putnam's Sons, 1966.

Knobel, Edward. *Field Guide to the Grasses, Sedges, and Rushes of the United States*. New York: Dover Publications, Inc., 1977, 1980.

Lane, Frenchman and Associates. "Elm Bank Master Plan." Boston: Massachusetts Division of Capital Planning and Operations, 1990.

Langtry, Albert P., Editor. *Metropolitan Boston, A Modern History*. New York: Lewis Historical Publishing Company, 1929.

Little, Elbert L. *The Audubon Society Field Guide to North American Trees*. New York: Alfred A. Knopf, 1980.

Mason, Orion T. *The Handbook of Medway History*. Medway, 1913.

Meserve, Clement. *History and Directory of Hopkinton, Massachusetts*. Needham: A.E. Foss & Company, 1891.

Partridge, George F. *History of the Town of Bellingham*. Bellingham: Town of Bellingham, 1919.

Peterson, Roger. *A Field Guide to the Birds*. Boston: Houghton Mifflin Company, 1980.

Pfeiffer, Marion. "The Morse Mills at South Natick, 1959."

Prescot, John R. *Suburban Living at its Best*. Newton: Newtonville Library Association, 1936.

River Guide Committee. *AMC River Guide, Massachusetts, Connecticut, Rhode Island*. Boston: Appalachian Mountain Club, 1985.

Russell, Howard S. *Indian New England Before the Mayflower*. Hanover, New Hampshire and London, England: University Press of New England, 1980.

Rutman, Darrett B. *Winthrop's Boston*. New York: W.W. Norton & Company, 1965.

Sanders, John E. *Principles of Physical Geology*. New York: John Wiley & Sons, 1981.

Shaughnessy, Anne Carr. *The History of Sherborn*. Sherborn: The 300th Anniversary Committee, 1974.

Smith, Frank. *A History of Dedham, Massachusetts.* Dedham: 1936.

Smith, Frank. *Dover Farms.* Dover Historical and Natural History Society, 1914.

Smith, Frank. *A History of Dover, Massachusetts.* Dover: Town of Dover, 1897.

Stokes, Donald W. *Guide to Bird Behavior, Volume I.* Boston: Little, Brown, and Company, 1979.

Stokes, Don and Lillian. *A Guide to Bird Behavior, Volume II.* Boston: Little, Brown, and Company, 1983.

Sweetser, M.F. *King's Handbook of Newton, Massachusetts.* Boston: Moses King Corporation, 1889.

Three Hundredth Anniversary Committee. *Mendon, Massachusetts.* Mendon: Mendon Historical Society, 1967.

Tilden, William S. *History of the Town of Medfield, Massachusetts.* Boston: George H. Ellis, 1887.

Tourtellot, Arthur Bernon. *The Charles.* New York: Farrar and Rinehart, 1941.

United States Army Corps of Engineers. *Charles River Natural Valley Storage Project Master Plan.* Waltham: United States Army Corps of Engineers, New England Division, 1984.

Walling, Henry F. "Map of Norfolk County, Massachusetts". Boston, 1853.

Webber, Margo. *Charles River 1987 Water Quality and Wastewater Discharge Data.* Westborough: Massachusetts Division of Water Pollution Control, 1988.

Weinstein-Farson, Laurie. *The Wampanoag.* New York: Chelsea House Publishers, 1989.

Winslow, Ola Elizabeth. *John Eliot, Apostle to the Indians.* Boston: Houghton Mifflin Company, 1968.

Zen, E-an, Editor. "Bedrock Geologic Map of Massachusetts". Reston, Virginia: United States Geological Survey, 1983.

Acknowledgements

Ed Kiniry of the Stowe Canoe Company lent two Allagash canoes, one solo and one tandem, for the research of this book. The trim lines of these Endurance models made it easy to cover a lot of water, which helped me make the best use of my canoeing time.

I thank those who shared their knowledge of the Charles River with me: Steve Bassett of The Trustees of Reservations; Thomas D. Cabot, author of *Quickwater and Smooth*; geologist James Cahoon; and Francis Donovan, Medway author and historian. Also, Dan Driscoll and Karl Haglund, Planners, Metropolitan District Commission; Richard Heidebrecht of the Army Corps of Engineers; William Hogarth of West Roxbury, and Robert B. Hanson, Executive Director of the Dedham Historical Society. Also, Paul Hurd, President of the Medfield Historical Society; Peter Kastner of the Newton Conservators; Franklin King of the Sherborn Forest and Trails Association and the Charles River Watershed Association; Elissa Landre, Director of Massachusetts Audubon Society's Broadmoor Wildlife Sanctuary; Eleisha Lee, of the Dover Historical Society; and geologist Bill Miller. Also, John Monroe, former Executive Director of the Charles River Watershed Association; Robert J. Murphy, President of the West Roxbury Historical Society; Henry C. Papuga, Manager of the Milford Water Company; geologist Margaret Thompson of Wellesley College; Rick Toubeau of Franklin; and Margo Webber, the Charles River expert at the Division of Water Pollution Control of the Massachusetts Department of Environmental Protection.

This book benefitted from the suggestions of those who read the manuscript, and for this service I thank botanist Ray Angelo; Steve Basset; ornithologist Brad Blodgett of the Massachusetts Division of Fisheries and Wildlife; Cecile Costine; Dan Driscoll; Francis Donovan; and Barbara Luedtke, Department of Anthropology, UMass Boston. Also, Judy Mack; Barbara Mackey; Steve Morrissey; Lisa Standley; Margaret Thompson; Sally and Jed Watters; Margo Webber; and Keith Yocum.

I am especially grateful to Barbara Mackey, whose ideas improved this book and helped to shape its predecessor, *The Concord, Sudbury, and Assabet Rivers.*

Thanks to Peter Kallander, who flew me over the Charles on a crystal clear October day; to Cliff Hauptman, whose sonar-equipped boat probed the underwater topography of Populatic Pond; and to Henry R. Guild, Jr., who supported the illustrations.

Finally, thanks to those who shared my canoe, and braved frequent loss of steering while I made notes: Jon Klein, with whom I canoed most of the Charles, Leonard Gerwick, Paul Atwood, Barbara Mackey, Brian Cassie, Debbie and Molly McAdow, and Colin Reid.

Index

222

Ron McAdow

Ron McAdow grew up in Illinois, and after graduation from the University of Chicago, he moved to Massachusetts. He spent six years in Holliston, making animated films for children's television. His award-winning films *Hank the Cave Peanut* and *Captain Silas* are featured in library film screenings across the nation.

After working in environmental education in Texas for three years, in 1980 Ron returned to Massachusetts and for several years lived in Millis, at Blythebrook Farm, on the banks of Bogastow Brook. He now resides in Southborough with his wife Deborah Costine, who is a puppeteer, and their daughter Molly.

Ron is the author of *The Concord, Sudbury, and Assabet Rivers,* and *New England Time Line.* He is the director of YMCA Camp Lawrence on Bear Island in Meredith, New Hampshire.

Gordon Morrison

Artist/illustrator Gordon Morrison has an impressive and diverse list of accomplishments. Among them are books such as *Newcomb's Wildflower Guide, Field Guide to New England Forests* (one of several Gordon has done in the Peterson's Field Guide Series), *The Birdwatcher's Companion,* and *Ceremonial Times.* His work has also appeared in a number of periodicals including *Horticulture, The Curious Naturalist, Country Journal,* and *Backpacker.*

He has done dioramas as exhibition work for the Missouri Botanical Gardens, Boston Zoological Society, Public Service Company of New Hampshire, and the Massachusetts Audubon Society.

Gordon's fine art paintings have been collected and exhibited extensively throughout New England. A native of the Boston area, Gordon attended the School of the Museum of Fine Arts Boston, and graduated from the Butera School of Art.

Gordon and his wife Nancy live in North Attleborough, Massachusetts with their three children.